Studying Christianity

A series of introductory guides, books in the *Studying World Religions* series are designed as study aids for those approaching the world's religions for the first time.

Also available:

Studying Islam, Clinton Bennet

Forthcoming:
Studying Hinduism, David Ananda Hart
Studying Judaism, Melanie J. Wright

Studying
Christianity

William H. Brackney

continuum

Continuum International Publishing Group
The Tower Building   80 Maiden Lane
11 York Road   Suite 704
London SE1 7NX   New York NY 10038

www.continuumbooks.com

British Library Cataloguing-in-Publication Data
A catalogue record for this book is available from the British Library.

ISBN: HB: 978-0-8264-9885-4
        PB: 978-0-8264-9886-1

Library of Congress Cataloging-in-Publication Data
Brackney, William H.
Studying Christianity/William Brackney.
   p. cm.
Includes bibliographical references and index.
ISBN 978-0-8264-9886-1 – ISBN 978-0-8264-9885-4
1. Christianity–Study and teaching. I. Title.

BR121.3.B73 2009
230–dc22   2009017292

Typeset by Newgen Imaging Systems Pvt Ltd., Chennai, India
Printed and bound in Great Britain by CPI Antony Rowe,
Chippenham, Wiltshire

Dedicated to Rev. Dr. Millard R. Cherry, Theologian, Friend, and
first Principal of Acadia Divinity College
Whose questions have deepened my insights

Contents

Series Preface
Religious Studies and Critical Enquiry: Toward a New Relationship

Clinton Bennett

Birth of a discipline

This new series takes the view that, as a field of studies, the Study of Religion is multidisciplinary and poly-methodological and needs to not merely affirm this but to translate this claim into practice. Religious Studies has its academic, historical roots within faculties or departments of Theology, where it began as a Comparative Study of Religions predicated on the assumption that Christianity was either a model, or a superior religion. The first University appointment was in 1873, when William Fairfield Warren became Professor of Comparative Theology and of the History and Philosophy of Religion at Boston University. The concept of Christianity as a model meant that any-thing that qualified as a religion ought to resemble Christianity. Traditional subdivisions of Christian Studies, usually called Theology, were applied to all religious systems. Thus, a religion would have a founder, a scripture or scriptures, doctrines, worship, art, sacred buildings, and various rituals associated with the human life cycle. These elements could be identified, and studied, in any religion. This approach has obvious methodological advantages but it can end up making all religions look remarkably similar to each other and of course also to what serves as the template or model, that is, to Christianity. The very terms "Hinduism" and "Buddhism" were of European origin, since all religions had to be "isms" with coherent belief structures. The assumption that Christianity was somehow superior, perhaps uniquely true, or divinely revealed to the exclusion of other religions meant that other religions had to be understood either as human constructs or as having a more sinister origin. Theology was thus concerned with evaluation and with truth claims. The study of religions other than Christianity often aimed to demonstrate how these religions fell short of the Christian ideal. Their strengths and weaknesses were delineated. Some classified religions according to their position on a supposed evaluative scale, with the best at the top and the worst at the bottom. Religious Studies, as it developed as a distinctive field of study, quickly distanced itself from Theology even when taught within Theology departments. It would be mainly descriptive.

The break from theology

Evaluation would be left to theology. Assessing where a religion might be considered right or wrong, strong or weak might occupy a theologian but the student of religion would describe what he or she saw, regardless of their own opinion or lack of an opinion about whether religions have any actual link with a supra-human reality. Partly, this stemmed from Religious Studies' early interest in deconstructing religions. This was the attempt to determine how they began. Usually, they were understood as a response to, or products of, particular social and political contexts. This took the field closer to the social sciences, which remain neutral on such issues as the existence of God or whether any religion can claim to have been revealed, focusing instead on understanding how religions operate, either in society or psychologically. Incidentally, the term "Comparative Religion" has been used as a neutral term, that is, one that does not imply a comparison in order to refute or evaluate. In its neutral sense, it refers to the cataloging of religious data under thematic headings, such as ritual, myth, beliefs without any attempt to classify some as better than others. The field has, to a degree, searched for a name. Contenders include the Scientific Study of Religion, the History of Religion (or *Religionge-schichteschule*, mainly in the German-speaking academy) but since the founding of the pioneering department of Religious Studies, at Lancaster University under Ninian Smart in 1967, Religious Studies has become the preferred description especially in secular institutions. One issue has been whether to use "religion" in the plural or singular. If the singular is used, it implies that different religions belong to the same category. If the plural is used, it could denote the opposite, that they share nothing in common, arise from unrelated causes and have no more to do with each other than, say, the Chinese and the Latin scripts, except that the former are beliefs about the divine-human relationship or the purpose of life while the latter are alphabets. Geo Widengren, professor of the History of Religion at Uppsala, rejected the notion that an *a priori, sui generis* phenomenon called "religion" existed as breaking the rules of objective, neutral, value-free scholarship. Incidentally, Buddhism and Confucianism were often characterized as philosophies, not as religions because they lacked a God or Gods at their center. On the history of the field, see Capps (1995) and Sharpe (2006).

Privileging insidership

The field soon saw itself as having closer ties to the humanities and to social science than to theology. It would be a multidisciplinary field, drawing on anthropology, psychology, philosophy, as well as on linguistics and literary criticism to study different aspects of a religion, what people do as well as what they say they believe, their sacred texts, their rituals, their buildings as well as how they organize themselves. However, a shift occurred in the development of the discipline, or field of study since it is a multidisciplinary field, that effectively reduced the distance between itself, and theology, from which it had tried so hard to divorce itself. While claiming to be a multidisciplinary field, Religious Studies has in practice veered toward privileging a single approach, or way of studying religion, above others. The shift toward what may be called phenomenology or insider-ship took place for good reasons and as a much-needed corrective to past mistakes and distortions. In the postcolonial space, much criticism has been voiced about how the Western world went about the task of studying the religious and cultural Other. Here, the voice of Edward Said is perhaps the most widely known. Much scholarship, as Said (1978) argued, was placed at the service of Empire to justify colonial rule and attitudes of racial or civilizational superiority. Such scholars, known as Orientalists, said Said, described Others, whether Africans, native Americans, Hindus or Muslims, Arabs or Chinese, who, so that they could be dominated, were inalienably different from and inferior to themselves. However, this description did not correspond to any actual reality. The term "Other" is widely used in postcolonial discourse and in writing about Alterity to refer to those who are different from us. The term was first used by Hegel. In contemporary use, it denotes how we stigmatize others, so that all Muslims or all Hindus, or all Africans share the same characteristics that are radically different from and less desirable than our own. Cabezón (2006) argues, "the dialectic of alterity is as operative today in the discipline of religious studies as it was in the discipline's antecedents." This is a sobering assessment (21). The Orientalists portrayed the non-Western world as chaotic, immoral, backward, and as exotic, as sometimes offering forbidden fruits but always offering adventure, riches, and the opportunity to pursue a career as a colonial administrator, in the military, in commerce, or even as a Christian missionary. Religions were often depicted as idolatrous, superstitious, oppressive, and as the source of much social evil.

Admittedly, some scholars, including the man who can be credited as founding the scientific study of religion, F. Max Müller, thought that religions such as Hinduism and Buddhism had become corrupt over time and that in their most ancient, original form they represented genuine apprehensions of divine truth. Writing in 1892, he remarked that if he seemed to speak too well of these religions there was little danger of the public "forming too favorable an opinion of them" since there were many other writers who presented their "dark and hideous side" (78). It was in his *Chips from a German Workshop* (1867) that Müller used the term "scientific study of religion." Supposition about the human origin of religion, perhaps excluding Christianity, resulted in a range of theories about how religions began. Britain's first professor of Comparative Religion, T. W. Rhys-Davids of Manchester thought that his work on the classical texts would help to separate the rational, ethical core of Buddhism from the myths and legends that surrounded its contemporary practice. Often, the socialpolitical and cultural milieu in which a founder type figure could be located were regarded as significant contributory factors. In the case of Hinduism, the "lack of a founder" was often commented upon almost as if this alone detracted from the possibility that Hinduism was a *bone fide* faith. Even such a careful scholar as Whaling says that Hinduism lacks a founder (1986: 43). In the case of Islam, Muhammad was invariably depicted as the author of the Qur'an and as Islam's founder, neither of which reflect Muslim conviction. Of course, for Christian polemicists, Muhammad was a charlatan and worse, Hinduism was a tissue of falsehood and Buddhism, if it qualified as a religion at all, was selfish! The result of this approach was to deconstruct religion, to reduce religion to something other than revealed truth. Instead, religion was a psychological prop or a sociological phenomenon that helps to police societies or a political tool used by the powerful to subdue the poor. Another aspect was that ancient or classical rather than contemporary religion was the main subject matter of religious studies.

The personal dimension

Even before Said, in reaction to the above, a different approach began to dominate the field. Partly, this was motivated by a desire—not absent in

Müller—to right some of the wrongs committed as a result of what can only be described as racial bias. One of the most important contributors to the new approach was Wilfred Cantwell Smith who, in 1950 in his own inaugural lecture as professor of Comparative Religion at McGill, spoke of the earlier generation of scholars as resembling "flies crawling on the surface of a goldfish bowl, making accurate observations on the fish inside ... and indeed contributing much to our knowledge of the subject; but never asking themselves, and never finding out, how it feels to be a goldfish" (2).[1] Scholars such as Gerardus van der Leeuw (1890–1950), influenced by the philosophical concept of phenomenology, had already applied its principles to religious studies, arguing that the field should move beyond description, "an inventory and classification of the phenomena as they appear in history" to an attempt to understand "all the experiences born of what can only become reality after it has been admitted into the life of the believer" (1954: 10). This introduced what Smith called a personal element into the study of religion, an element that has always played a part in theology, which deals with matters of faith, with people's most cherished and deeply held convictions. Smith suggested that all religions should be understood in personal terms: religion is "the faith in men's hearts"; it is "a personal thing, in the lives of men" (1959: 42). Thus the student will make progress when he or she recognizes that they are not primarily dealing with externals, with books and rituals that can be observed but with "religious persons, or at least with something interior to persons" (1959: 53). In the past, the study of "other men's religions" had taken the form of an "impersonal presentation of an 'it'" (1959: 34). Now, instead of an "us" talking about "them," it would first become "us" talking "to them," then a "'we all' talking with each other about 'us'" as Religious Studies took on the task of interpreting "intellectually the cosmic significance of life generically, not just for one's own group specifically" (1981: 187). The Religious Studies' professor now wrote for the Other as well as for outsiders, since they would also read what he wrote. "The day has long past," said Smith, "when we write only for ourselves" (1981: 143). Phenomenology, applied to the study of religions, is the effort to penetrate to the essential core, to the *eidos*, of religion, by bracketing out assumptions, theories, preconceptions so that we see the phenomenon for what it really is, in its own terms. Instead of imposing categories and theories and value judgments from outside, like the Orientalists did, we enter into the religion's worldview. We all but become the Other. Instead of decrying what we write as a mockery, as inaccurate, as belittling what he or she believes, the Other ought to voice their approval (1959: 44).

Leaving aside the problem that not all Muslims or all Hindus or all Buddhists believe identically and that what one believer finds acceptable another may not, nonetheless, the criterion that believers should recognize themselves in what gets written, has become a generally accepted principle within Religious Studies. It is also widely embraced in anthropology. Certainly, effort is made to represent religions as diverse, to counter the impression given by earlier writers that Islam, for example, was more or less the same everywhere and, for that matter, throughout history. Smith himself insisted that there is actually no such thing as Hinduism or as Christianity or as Islam, only what this Hindu or that Muslim believes. At the deepest level, this is undoubtedly true. However, Religious Studies would not survive if it took this too literally, so pragmatically it accepts that while no abstract reality called "Christianity" or "Islam" may exist, believers also believe that they belong to a religious tradition and share beliefs with others who belong to that tradition. They believe that these are not merely their own, individual personal opinions but are "true," that is, according to the teachings of the religion itself. The phenomenological approach, or methodology, then, tries to depict a religion in terms that insiders recognize. Thus, when explaining how a religion began, it describes what believers themselves hold to be true. An outsider writing about Islam might attribute its origin to Muhammad's genius in responding to the need for political unity in seventh-century Arabia by supplying a religion as the unifying creed that bound rival tribes together. The phenomenologist will write of how Muhammad received the Qur'an from God via the Angel Gabriel in a cave on Mt. Hira in the year 610 of the Common Era. The phenomenologist does not have to ask, unlike a theologian, whether Muhammad really did receive revelation. However, by neglecting other explanations of Islam's origin they veer, if not toward theology then at least toward a type of faith sensitivity that is closer to that of a theologian than to a Freudian psychologist or a Durkheimian sociologist.

Faith sensitivity: A paradigm too far

From at least the mid-1970s, what has been taught in most College and University departments of Religious Studies or in world religions courses within departments of Theology or of Religion is the phenomenology of religion. Most popular texts on the religions of the world depict their subject matter in what can be described as an insider-sensitive style. Indeed, there is a tendency to employ Hindus to teach about Hinduism, Muslims to teach about

Islam, so what gets taught represents a fairly standard and commonly accepted Hindu or Muslim understanding of these faiths. Hinduism does not get described as having kept millions of people in bondage to the evils of the caste or class system, nor is Islam depicted as an inherently violent religion, or as misogynist. This tendency to appoint insiders has meant, in practice, little of the type of collaboration, or "colloquy" that Smith anticipated (1981: 193) but also much less misrepresentation. Partly, the trend stems from the suspicion that it takes one to know one. In anthropology, Clifford Geertz has spoken of an "epistemological hypochondria concerning how one can know that anything one says about other forms of life is as a matter of fact so" (1988: 71). There is a reluctance to depict all religions as basically the same or to imply that the same fundamental truths can be found in all of them—if differently expressed—because this sounds like theology. However, a similar pedagogical approach to teaching each tradition is commonly practiced. While this approach is more sophisticated than the early model, which simply used Christianity as a template, it is not so radically different. Here, the work of Ninian Smart and Frank Whaling, among others, has been influential (Figure 0.1). Sharpe's "four modes of religion" model is worth examining but is less easy to translate into the classroom (see Figure 0.2). Smart and Whaling say that most religions have such elements as beliefs, scriptures, histories, sacred sites, worship and that without imposing too much from the outside, an examination of each of these provides a common framework of investigation. Smart's term "worldview," too, easily includes Marxism as well as Buddhism, and is less problematic than religion because no belief in the supernatural is implied. Flexibility is possible because some traditions place more stress on certain elements; therefore, these can be discussed in more detail. The role, for example, of a seminal personality in Islam, Christianity, or Buddhism is very significant while less so in Judaism and absent in Hinduism. One very positive development associated with this personal understanding of religion was that the field started to take an interest in contemporary religion, not only in ancient texts. Observation and fieldwork, alongside knowledge of languages and literary analysis, became part and parcel of studying religion. If anything, the trend may have gone too far in the other direction, to the neglect of texts. It is just as mistaken to think that you can learn all about a religion by visiting a place of worship as it is to claim that everything can be learnt from reading its texts. It is not insignificant that when Smart proposed his original six dimensions it was in the context of a lecture on the "Nature of Theology and the Idea of A Secular University," thus his concern was with the "logic of

Smart's seven-fold scheme of study (initially six; see Smart, 1968: 15–18).	Whaling's eight inter-linked elements, behind which lies some apprehension of ultimate reality (Whaling, 1986: 37–48).
1. Doctrinal	1. Religious community
2. Mythological	2. Ritual
3. Ethical	3. Ethics
4. Ritual	4. Social involvement
5. Historical	5. Scriptures/myth
6. Social	6. Concepts
7. Material (added in his 1998 text)	7. Aesthetics
	8. Spirituality

Note: Smart categorized 1–3 as "para-historical" and 4–6 as historical.

Figure 0.1 Comparison of Smart's and Whaling's models.

religious education in a secular or religiously neutralist society . . . with the *content* of what should be taught" rather than with the "question of *how* religion should be taught" (1968: 7).

This series takes the view that phenomenology or insider-sensitivity dominates the field today at the expense of other ways of studying religion. This series also takes the view that this dominance has cost Religious Studies its ability to engage with critical issues. The reality of what a student experiences in the field may be different, less pleasant, than what they learn in the classroom. From what is taught in the classroom, religions are all sweetness and light. True, the darker side of religion may indeed be a distortion, or a misrepresentation, or the result of the manipulation of religion for political or for other ends. True, the earliest strand of the religion may not have contained these elements. However, to say nothing about how a religion has been used to sanction, even to bless violence, or to subjugate women, or to discriminate against outsiders or certain designated groups, simply reverses the mistakes of the past. If the Orientalists rarely had anything good to say about religions other than the Christian, the contemporary student of religion appears blind to anything negative. One of the most popular Religious Studies texts, at least in North America, is Huston Smith's *The World's Religions* (1958; 1991; originally *The Religions of Man*). For all its merit, this deliberately set out to present religions as sweetness and light, or, as the author put it, to show religions "at their best" (5). Smith himself winced to think how someone closing his chapter on Hinduism and stepping "directly into the Hinduism

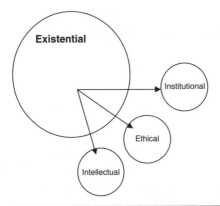

Sharpe sees these as interlinking. Each can be represented by a noun: Existential = faith; Intellectual = beliefs; Institutional = Organizations; Ethical = conduct. A believer or a community may use either of the four as the 'dominant element', that as, as a 'gateway' to the others (p97). On page 96, he has four diagrams, substituting the dominant dimension in each.

Figure 0.2 Eric Sharpe's "four-modes." *Source:* Based on diagram on page 96 in Sharpe, 1983.

described by Nehru as 'a religion that enslaves you'" would react (4). He excluded references to the Sunni-Shi'a and traditional-modernist divisions in Islam (3) because he chose instead to note "different attitudes toward Sufism" by way of taking Islam's diversity seriously. Yet this also avoided discussing some less rose-colored aspects of religion, the full story of which is "not rose-colored" but "often crude" (4). What Smith set out to achieve may be said to characterize the Religious Studies' agenda; he wanted to "penetrate the worlds of the Hindus, the Buddhists, and Muslims" and to "throw bridges from these worlds" to his readers. His goal was "communication" (10). He wrote of aiming to see through "others' eyes" (8). Toward the end of his "Points of Departure" chapter explaining his methodology, he gives an eloquent description of phenomenology, which, although he does not call it that, is worth repeating:

> First, we need to see their adherents [World religions' adherents] as men and women who faced problems much like our own. Secondly, we must rid our minds of all preconceptions that could dull our sensitivity or alertness to fresh insights. If we lay aside our preconceptions about these religions, seeing each as forged by people who were struggling to see something that would give help and meaning to their lives; and if we then try without prejudice to see ourselves what they see—if we do these things, the veil that separates us from them can turn to gauze (11).

Smart describes the process as one of "structured empathy," a crossing over of "our horizons into the worlds of other people" (1983: 16).

Avoiding the less "rosy"

Yet by ignoring such problematic an issue as the Sunni-Shi'a division in Islam, Smith's book, as admirable as it is, provides no tools that could help someone trying to make sense of events in Lebanon, in Iran, and in Iraq. Arguably, this reluctance to deal with critical issues results from over sensitivity to insider sensibilities. A theologian may justify elevating faith sensitivity over all alternatives but if Religious Studies is a social science, other, less faith sensitive explanations and content should also be given space on the curriculum. A faith sensitive treatment of Christianity, for example, would depict Jesus as the son of God and as the second person of the Trinity, who died and rose again, replicating what Christians believe. The implication here is not that it can be stated as fact that Jesus died and rose again but that this is what Christians believe. However, a critical approach might take Jesus' humanity as a starting point and try to understand the process by which belief in his divinity developed. Christian scholars themselves explore the degree to which the words of Jesus in the Gospels may reflect the convictions of the primitive Christian community, rather than what Jesus really said. Yet this rarely intrudes into a Religious Studies class on Christianity. The volume on Christianity in this series, however, examines the problem of canonicity and discusses the existence of later gospels and epistles as a case for a variegated Christian tradition in the first three centuries. Similarly, a faith sensitive explanation of Muhammad's career depicts him as the sinless prophet of God, who contributed nothing to the content of the Qur'an, replicating what Muslims believe. Again, the implication here is not that it can be stated as a fact that Muhammad received the Qur'an from God but that Muslims believe that he did. However, an alternative view of Muhammad might regard him as someone who sincerely believed that God was speaking to him and whose own ideas and perhaps those of some of his companions found expression, consciously or unconsciously, in Islam's scripture and teachings. Such an alternative view does not have to follow the pattern of past anti-Muslim polemic, in which Muhammad was a charlatan, an opportunist, insincere and self-serving. Kenneth Cragg, who has contributed much to helping Christians form a more sympathetic view of Islam, sees Muhammad as a sincere servant of God but he does not think that the Qur'an contains nothing of

Muhammad's own ideas. Cragg, though, may be regarded as a theologian rather than as belonging properly to Religious Studies, which begs the question whether it is useful to maintain a distinction between these two fields. Suggesting how outsiders, who wish to remain committed members of a different faith, can approximate an insider-like view without compromising their own could be part of the agenda of Religious Studies. Currently, this role appears to be undertaken by practitioners of interfaith dialog, such as Hans Küng (see Küng, 1986) and by theologians such as Cragg, rather than by Religious Studies specialists. In many instances, the distinction is blurred because of the different roles played by people themselves. Frank Whaling is not only a Religious Studies specialist but also an ordained Methodist minister. W. C. Smith was a Religious Studies specialist (although he preferred the term Comparative Religion) but was an ordained Presbyterian minister. Methodist minister, Kenneth Cracknell had contributed significantly to thinking on how to understand the relationships between religions but it is difficult to say whether his academic credentials identify him as a theologian or as a Religious Studies specialist (see Cracknell, 1986; 2006). The same can probably be said of this writer. Cabezón discusses the acceptability of scholars today declaring their faith allegiances in relation to the "us" and "them" divide, pointing out that some scholars "self-identify as belonging to multiple religious traditions" and so a simplistic "us" and "them" polarity is problematic; "the Other is problematic when *we* claim to BE-THEM" (33). The author of the volume on Buddhism in this series, the topic of his doctorate, was born a Hindu, became Christian but self-identifies as a Hindu-Christian. The author of the volume on Hinduism regards himself as a Hindu but continues to be a licensed priest of the Church of England, a fact that has attracted some criticism in the British press. How will Religious Studies deal with such complexities?[2]

Discussion of some alternative explanations and critical theories can be problematic, given that believers may find them offensive. Some scholars who have challenged the Muslim consensus on Islam's origins have received death threats, so replicating insider views is less risky. A teacher who wants to attract insider approval may find it expedient to ignore other views. The possibility that material from the Gnostic gospels can be identified in the Qur'an, for example, runs contrary to Muslim conviction, and is ignored by almost everyone except Christian polemicists. A Muslim in the classroom may be offended if the teacher alludes to this type of source and redaction critical approach to the Qur'an. Such an approach, if it is pursued, may take place elsewhere in the academy. What has been described as shattering the "consensus of scholarly opinion on the origins of Islam" came from outside the corridors of any Department of Religion or of Religious Studies (Neuwirth, 2006: 100). The Aryan invasion theory is increasingly unpopular among Hindus, who dismiss it as imperialist. This Euro-centric theory, it is said, denies that India's heritage is really Indian. Yet, to ignore the relationship between Indian and European languages and the similarity of some ideas and myths could be to overlook important facts about a more interconnected human story than is often supposed. On the one hand, the term "Hinduism" is now accepted by many Hindus. On the other hand, its appropriateness can be challenged. Smith commented, "the mass of religious phenomena we shelter under that umbrella is not an entity in any theoretical let alone practical sense" (1963: 64). As taught, Hinduism arguably owes more to the Theosophist, Annie Bessant, who may have been the first to design a curriculum based around the four aims in life, four ages, the four stages of life and the four classes and their duties than to any classical Indian text, even though all these can be found in the texts. The elevation of a great tradition over the myriad of smaller traditions needs to be critiqued. Western fascination with Hinduism's esoteric system, Tantra, has attracted criticism that this elevates what is actually quite obscure to a seemingly more central position. Since sex is involved, this revives a certain Orientalist preoccupation with the East as alluring and immoral, offering possibilities for pleasure denied by the West. Wendy Doniger O'Flaherty, a former President of the American Academy of Religion, has been criticized for overstressing sensuality in her work on Hinduism (see Ramaswamy et al., 2007).

What has been described as Protestant Buddhism, too, developed as a result of the efforts of another Theosophist, Henry Steele Olcott, among others. A type of "philosopher's abstraction" (Gombrich, 1988: 50) it set out to present Buddha's teaching as a coherent, systematic system, beginning with the four noble truths followed by the noble eightfold path. These were taught by the Buddha but he loved lists, and these are two among many. This is not to suggest that Buddhism is unsystematic, although use of the term "systematic" here could be another example of transposing a European concept into non-European space. In fact, believing that people at different spiritual stages require different teachings, the Buddha sometimes gave different advice on the same issue. Teaching that may appear contradictory, as the fourteenth Dalai Lama put it, prevents "dogmatism" (1996: 72). It could be argued, then, that the somewhat dogmatic way in which what the Buddha taught is presented in many Religious Studies classrooms, misrepresents what he actually taught. Kitagawa (1959) observed, and arguably not much has changed, that "despite its avowed neutrality and objectivity," Religious Studies "has been operating with Western categories" (27). More recently, Cabezón has said that Religious Studies is still dominated by Western terms, theories, and paradigms. Theory parity, says Cabezón, is a long way off; "for example, it is hard for us to even conceive of the day when a "Theories of religion" course might be taught with a substantial selection of readings from nonwestern sources" (31). How long are Western views of religion and of what is to be included and excluded as religiously interesting going to dominate? Cabezón identifies at least the start of a much needed paradigm shift in which non-Western theologies are getting some exposure (34). Cabezón also argues that some non-Buddhist scholars, despite the insider-ship bias of the discipline, "still construct their identity in contradistinction to the Buddhist Other" which effectively emphasizes the distance between themselves and the "object (Buddhism)" they choose to study (29 Fn 22). The volume on Judaism discusses problems associated with the very definition of Judaism as a religion, and the relationship between Judaism and the Jewish people, often assumed to be identical. It asks whether such a significant thinker as Freud, who was secular, can be located within a Jewish religious framework. The same question could be asked of Marx.

Another issue, relevant to studying and teaching all religions on the curriculum, is how much should realistically be attempted. If a degree is offered in Islamic Studies, or Buddhist Studies, or Jewish Studies, this issue is less relevant. However, more often than not, what gets taught is a survey course covering five or six religions. If a traditional course in Christian Studies covers scripture, history, philosophy of religion, theology, and languages, the student usually has 3 or 4 years to master these. In a survey course, they have perhaps a day to master a religion's scripture, another day to study its historical development, another to gain an understanding of its rituals. It is widely recognized that in order to understand another world view, some grasp of language is necessary, given the difficulty of translating meaning across languages. Muslims, indeed, say that the Qur'an is untranslatable, that it is only God's word in Arabic. How much Hebrew, how much Arabic, how much Sanskrit, can students be expected to learn in a few days? If the answer is "hardly any," are they really able to achieve anything that approximates insider-ship? It is often claimed that students learn more from attending a service of worship than they do from books. This writer has taken students to

Mosques where quite hostile attempts to convert them to Islam left them with a less positive view of Islam than they had taken away from the classroom. Yet can any course on Islam neglect a mosque visit? This author has chosen to leave one out on the basis that no such course can cover everything anyway! Another issue, also relevant to studying all traditions covered on the curriculum, is how different interpretations of texts are to be dealt with. For example, the Qur'an can be read by militants as permitting aggression, by others as prohibiting aggression and sanctioning only defense. Can both be right? Is it the business of so-called neutral Religious Studies scholars, who may well be located in a secular and possibly public (State) school, to say what is, or is not, a more authentic version of Judaism, of Islam, or of Christianity? In some contexts, this could even raise issues of Church-State relations. How seriously should a Religious Studies specialist take the postmodern view that all texts have multiple meanings and no single reading can claim to be exclusively or uniquely true? This certainly challenges some religious voices, which claim infallibility or at least to speak with special, privileged authority! Far from being fixed objects, or subjects of study, religions are often in flux. The Christian volume, for example, shows how ethical thinking on such issues as war and peace, justice, economic distribution, and human sexuality has changed over time and varies across Christian communities.

Reviving critical enquiry

If Religious Studies is to live up to its claim to be a social science, it cannot afford to ignore other approaches and critical issues, even if these are less-faith sensitive. Otherwise, it must resign itself to merely describing what believers themselves hold to be true. Only by placing alternative approaches alongside insider perspectives can Religious Studies claim to be treating religious beliefs and practices as subjects of serious and critical investigation. This is not to suggest that faith sensitivity should be abandoned. One reason why students study religions other than their own, or any religion for that matter, is to understand what believers really believe, often as opposed to how their beliefs are popularly or commonly portrayed. A religious studies' student may be an agnostic, or an atheist but he or she will still want to know what a Hindu or a Jew believes, not what some prejudiced outsider says about them. Stripping away misconceptions, overcoming bias and prejudice, presenting a religion from its believers' perspective, will remain an important goal of any Religious

Studies program. However, the privileging of insider-ship to the exclusion of other ways of seeing religion reduces Religious Studies to a descriptive exercise, and compromises any claim to be a critical field of academic enquiry. Religious Studies will be enriched, not impoverished, by reclaiming its multidisciplinary credentials. This series examines how issues and content that is often ignored in teaching about religions can be dealt with in the classroom. The aim is, on the one hand, to avoid giving unnecessary offence while on the other hand to avoid sacrificing critical scholarship at the altar of a faith-sensitivity that effectively silences and censures other voices. Since critical issues vary from religion to religion, authors have selected those that are appropriate to the religion discussed in their particular volume. The Smart-Whaling dimensional approach is used to help to give some coherency to how authors treat their subjects but these are applied flexibly so that square pegs are not forced into round holes. Each author pursues his/her enquiry according to his/her expert view of what is important for the tradition concerned, and of what will help to make Religious Studies a healthier, more critical field. Each author had the freedom to treat his/her subject as he/she chose, although with reference to the aim of this series and to the Smart-Whaling schema. What is needed is a new relationship between Religious Studies and critical enquiry. A balance between faith-sensitivity and other approaches is possible, as this series proves. These texts, which aim to add critical edge to the study of the religions of the world, aim to be useful to those who learn and to those who teach, if indeed that distinction can properly be made. Emphasis on how to tackle critical issues rather than on the content of each dimension may not make them suitable to use as introductory texts for courses as these have traditionally been taught. They might be used to supplement a standard text. Primarily aids to study, they point students toward relevant material including films and novels as well as scholarly sources.

They will, however, be very appropriate as textbooks for innovative courses that adopt a more critical approach to the subject, one that does not shy away from problematical issues and their serious, disciplined exploration.

References

Cabezón, José Ignacio. "The Discipline and its Others: The Dialectic of Alterity in the Study of Religion," *Journal of the American Academy of Religion*, 74: 1, 21–38, 2006.

Capps, Walter H. *Religious Studies: The Making of a Discipline*. Minneapolis, MN: Fortress Press, 1995.

Cracknell, Kenneth. *Towards a New Relationship: Christians and People of Other Faith.* London: Epworth, 1986.

Cracknell, Kenneth. *In Good and Generous Faith: Christian Responses to Religious Pluralism.* Cleveland, OH: The Pilgrim Press, 2006.

Dalai Lama, fourteenth. *The Good Heart: A Buddhist Perspective on the Teaching of Jesus.* Edited by Robert Kierly. Boston, MT: Wisdom Publications, 1996.

Geertz, Clifford. *Works and Lives: The Anthropologist as Author.* Stanford, CA: Stanford University Press, 1988.

Gombrich, Richard. *Therevada Buddhism.* London: Routledge, 1988.

Kitagawa, Joseph. "The history of religions in America," in M. Eliade and J. Kitagawa, editors. *The History of Religions: Essays in Methodology.* Chicago, IL: Chicago University Press, 1–30, 1959.

Küng, Hans. *Christianity and the World Religions.* London: SCM, 1986.

Leeuw, G. van der. "Confession Scientique," *NUMEN,* 1, 8–15, 1954.

Müller, F. Max. *Chips from a German Workshop.* London: Longmans & Co., 1867.

Müller, F. Max. *Introduction to the Science of Religion.* London: Longmans & Co., 1882.

Neuwirth, Angelika. "Structural, linguistic and literary features," in Jane Dammen McAuliffe, editor. *The Cambridge Companion to the Qur'an.* Cambridge: Cambridge University Press, 97–113, 2006.

Ramaswamy, Krishnan, de Nicholas, Antonio and Banerjee, Aditi, editors. *Invading the Sacred: An Analysis of Hinduism Studies in America.* Delhi: Rupa & Co., 2007.

Said, Edward. *Orientalism.* New York: Pantheon, 1978.

Sharpe, Eric J. *Understanding Religion.* London: Duckworth, 1983.

Sharpe, Eric J. *Comparative Religion: A History.* New Edition. London: Duckworth, 2006.

Smart, Ninian. *Secular Education and the Logic of Religion.* New York: Humanities Press, 1968.

Smart, Ninian. *Worldviews.* New York: Macmillan, 1983.

Smart, Ninian. *The World's Religions.* Cambridge: Cambridge University Press, 1998.

Smith, Huston. *The World's Religions.* San Francisco, CA: HarperSanFrancisco, 1958; 1991.

Smith, Wilfred Cantwell. *The Comparative Study of Religion: An Inaugural Lecture.* Montreal: McGill University, 1950.

Smith, Wilfred Cantwell. "Comparative Religion: Whither and Why?" in M. Eliade and J. Kitagawa, editors. *The History of Religions: Essays in Methodology.* Chicago, IL: Chicago University Press, 31–58, 1959, available online at http://www.religion-online.org/showchapter.asp?title=580&C=761h

Smith, Wilfred Cantwell. *The Meaning and End of Religion: A New Approach to the Religious Traditions of Mankind.* New York: Macmillan, 1963.

Smith, Wilfred Cantwell. *Towards a World Theology.* Philadelphia, PA: Westminster Press, 1981.

Whaling, Frank. *Christian Theology and World Religions: A Global Approach.* London: Marshall, Morgan & Scott, 1986.

Foreword

Each year as I prepare my Holocaust course, I wonder about the teaching of this event. How can I instruct my students about this most horrific event without trivializing it? I wonder, too, given the current state of our world, if the event has already been trivialized. In a world where Holocaust imagery pervades our culture and yet at the same time, violence and atrocity continue apace, is there any validity to reciting the lessons of the Holocaust when they aren't taken seriously, sometimes not even by Jews?

Of course, a main component of any study of the Holocaust is Christian anti-Semitism. My students, mostly Christian and often evangelical, bristle when they begin to learn of the underside of Christian history. I often think that they must have heard this story many, many times before. But, like the Holocaust, with Christian symbols pervading our culture, Christianity is often trivialized as well.

So it was quite surprising when I received this interesting manuscript, *Studying Christianity*. At first I wanted to place it in my desk drawer; as a Jew, especially when I am teaching the Holocaust, my feelings of ambivalence toward Christianity reach a crescendo. At the same time, I realize that the same students who resent my recounting of the sins of Christianity know very little of the Christian heritage, including the struggle to define exactly what it means to be a Christian. *Studying Christianity* might well be what they need to read.

Because of my studies of religion, I, of course, had indeed studied Christianity, but in reading this book I became reacquainted with the diverse dynamics of an ancient and global religion. Though my teaching of the Holocaust can only emphasize certain aspects of Christian history, Christianity's whole is better than its parts. Stated differently, the history of Christianity has so many twists and turns that its past can be seen as prologue. Depending on what road is taken, Christianity's past can be prologue for a new emphasis on life over death, a resurrection politics and economics that might lead us past the crucified Jews of the past and those who are victimized today as well.

Could my students have a better view of what their Christianity might be if they studied Christianity like they study the Holocaust? It seems that

Christianity, like any religion, should be studied alongside formative events in history. Studied in a dynamic way, as a force within and outside of history, but only known and embraced by us within the exigencies of history, perhaps Christians might then choose another path than was chosen before.

So it went for me during this season, teaching the Holocaust and reading *Studying Christianity* side by side. What I experienced is perhaps what other readers might also experience: following the arc of Christian history, I am struck by the sense that Christians believe that the world is redeemed—and has yet to be. I am also struck by the arguments for and against the peoples of the world, including the Jews, and how things can go so wrong that only darkness reigns and just when that night seems permanent, dawn arrives. We can think, learn, pray, and live with a new understanding of an original faith in the now context of our lives.

Christianity stands at a crossroads. Is there any other time in history where a Jew would be asked to write a short welcome to the readers of a book detailing the heritage and character of Christianity. *Studying Christianity* is part of the light, a heritage to be read, so that we, and the world, can be made new.

Marc H. Ellis, Ph.D.
University Professor of Jewish Studies and
Director of the Center for Jewish Studies
Baylor University, Waco, Texas, USA.

Acknowledgments

I have much enjoyed this project, in part because it grows out of teaching Christianity to a variety of students in various settings, theological schools, undergraduate and graduate programs in universities. I have attempted to be self-critical and yet appreciative of the landscape of the tradition of which I am a part. I have relied upon a vast number of scholars from various perspectives, only some of whom are reflected in the notes and bibliography. I trust I have faithfully reflected their contributions.

Throughout the text, the *New Revised Standard Version of the Bible* (NRSV) has been cited. It is used with permission of the National Council of Churches of Christ in the United States.

I am grateful to Tom Crick at Continuum Publishing and Clinton Bennett, the editor of this series, for their guidance and support. Dr. Bennett was formerly my colleague in the Department of Religion at Baylor University. My support from two libraries has been generous: that of Atlantic School of Theology in Halifax, and the Vaughan Library of Acadia University, for making materials and space available to me. I also wish to express my gratitude to the administration and trustees of Acadia Divinity College for the time to research and write, and to my wife, Kathryn, for her support and hearing of the manuscript.

William Brackney
William H. Brackney, B.A. (hons.), M.A.R., M.A., Ph.D.
The Millard R. Cherry Distinguished Professor of Christian Theology and Ethics and Director, Acadia Centre for Baptist and Anabaptist Studies Acadia Divinity College, Acadia University

Introduction:
Approaching Christianity

Jesus, the founder of Christianity, is depicted as one who regularly critiqued the Jewish religion, his ancestral religious orientation. At an early age, he was seen in the Jerusalem Temple debating the rabbis. Later in his adult ministry, he answered questions and publicly disputed the Pharisees, Sadducees, and Scribes. Jesus avoided strict interpretations of the Law in favor of principles of theology and ethics. He left a heritage of being one who taught with authority and one who welcomed interaction with seekers.

The first persons to examine Christianity after the life of Jesus were his disciples. From the interactions of Jesus with Peter, Thomas, and the dialog at his ascension among a group of disciples, there was an intensive debate about the meaning and applicability of Jesus' teachings. In the Book of Acts, the debate was frequently agitated, as the disagreement between Peter and Paul over dietary laws and required circumcision for the Christian community that James had to arbitrate. Other issues that created a healthy difference of opinion in the primitive Christian community included hierarchy of leadership, unusual manifestations of religious experience, and the priority of religious faith over works of merit.

By the time of the composition of the first literature of the New Testament, there were apparently several literary versions of the Christian witness in circulation. The writer of the Gospel of Luke said, "I investigated everything carefully from the very first, to write an orderly account . . ."[1] Likewise, the gospel authors Mark, Matthew, and John, and the apostle Paul each opened different windows on the meaning of the teachings of Jesus of Nazareth. It became the primary task of later collections of bishops and teachers (the Church "Fathers") to establish a uniform version of the Christian message and create an authoritative text of sacred writings that Christian refer to as the "canon" or standard of Scripture.

Eusebius of Caesarea (c.263–c.339) is joined by Tyrannius Rufinus (c.345–410), Socrates Scholasticus (380–439), Salminius Sozoman (c.390–c.457), Theodoret of Cyrrhus (c.393–c.458), and Evagrius Scholasticus (c.536–c.594) in providing the first historical analysis of Christianity. The historical discipline was important to the establishment of Christian learning because the historians traced the evolution of a tradition from the voluntary association of Jesus through the establishment of congregations in the Middle East, to the recognition of episcopacies or regional administrative units virtually throughout the Roman Empire. Eusebius attempted to cast Christianity over against the pagan cults and fit it into a narrative of human history that reached back to Creation. Sozomen, writing during the reign of Emperor Theodosius, extolled the virtues of imperial Christianity and the Christianization of the Roman Empire. Continuing the work of Eusebius, Rufinus blended the narratives of Eastern and Western Christianities and chronicled the development of monasticism in Egypt. Theodoret wrote a theological history of Christianity, seeking to identify and refute the Arian controversy from the standpoint of the school of theologians in Antioch. He understood the importance of the original sources and reproduced relevant documentation. Theodoret was also much impressed with reports of miraculous occurrences and gave numerous accounts of such experiences. Evagrius, also writing from Antioch, continued the narrative from the conclusions of his worthy predecessors and he dealt with the interaction of Christianity with barbarian people, giving his version a decidedly Eastern orientation, preserving many original sources. One of the most important achievements of the earliest historians of Christianity was their recognition of the regional diversity of the overall Christian tradition. One notes constant references to Asiatic Roman, African, and Palestinian types of Christian witness and thought. At the foundation of all early Christian scholarship was the historical enterprise, and it produced a surprisingly analytical accounting.

Theologians of the early church like Origen of Alexandria (185–c.254), the parent of systematic theological education, and Augustine (354–430), a widely published North African bishop, followed the lead of the Apostle Paul and moved Christian thought to a new level by practicing solid intellectual skills and by raising the correlation of faith and reason. Origen moved freely among extant philosophical schools, secular literature, physics, and ethics to blend an awareness of the divine with the world of human understanding. He dealt honestly with the seeming paradox between God's unity and the multiplicity of the material world, as well as the differences between first principles and nonrational impulses in making decisions. Among Origen's more controversial accomplishments was his allegorical method of interpreting scripture in order to derive multiple meanings from texts. Later, Augustine arrived at the position that God created the universe in God's sovereignty and therefore all of creation is thus dependent upon God. It then followed for Augustine that knowledge comes by way of a restored relationship with the Creator and that there is a purpose in human history and development that leads to fulfillment in God. Reflecting a three-in-one understanding of God, Augustine deduced that body, soul, and spirit compose the human self in the image of God. The heritages of both Origen and Augustine remain pervasive influences among the vast number of Christians presently as they respond to questions of knowledge, value, and morality.

Among the students of Christianity's character during the Middle Ages were regional historians like Bede of Northumbria (c.672–735) and the many chroniclers of the East. Bede's great accomplishment was to link the Christianization of Britain to the successive waves of monarchies and tribal confederations and demonstrate how a Christian culture had emerged. In the meantime, he happened to codify the English language in a form that would remain intact for centuries. In the Christian East, Saints Cyril and Methodius of Thessaloniki, Greece, are credited with a similar linguistic contribution in establishing the Cyrillic alphabet. In Kievan Rus, the family chronicles detail everyday interaction between villagers and priests and preserve an otherwise lost window on Orthodox medieval Christian experience. In addition to historians, monks and later members of the mendicant orders debated the meaning of the sacraments and church authority.

The capstone of Christian intellectual pursuits in the Middle Ages was Scholasticism, actually an attempt to use the methods of Aristotle to inquire into Christian faith and life. Leading thinkers in this movement, Anselm of Canterbury, Peter Abelard, Peter Lombard, Gratian, and Hugh of St. Victor, focused on a rigorous faith seeking understanding. Of all the scholastics, Thomas Aquinas at the University of Paris was foremost. These thinkers perfected a method of questions, the adduction of evidence and a reasoned conclusion to achieve a rational basis for the revealed truth of Christianity. Their bold assertions included several cogent arguments for the existence of God, a basis for the sacramental liturgy of Christian worship, and a body of principles called "natural law" to serve as a foundation for Christian ethics. Aquinas' unfinished work, the 70-volume *Summa Theologica* (1265–1274) and the structured curriculum of a new institution, the papally-chartered university, set the pattern for Christian learning for centuries to come. With Scholasticism, Christianity may truly be said to have come of age as a religious tradition.

The humanist movement in Europe during the Renaissance brought major scholarly attention to Christianity. The spirit of the Renaissance was devoted to an emphasis upon human beings and their circumstances, including their relation to God. In examining the "humanities," these scholars rejected the medieval synthesis of ecclesiastical authority in temporal as well as spiritual matters and Scholasticism, preferring instead to follow an intellectual combination of St. Augustine, Plato, and several Latin literati like Cicero. Francesco Petrarch (1304–1374) of Italy was the leader of the southern European Renaissance with an interest in the classical tradition of learning and the arts. The new learning also had a German and French phase that emerged in the late fifteenth century. Where such principles were applied to Christian thought and sources, it meant a rigorous textual recovery of ancient manuscripts in which the "true Christ" could be revealed without the overlay of metaphysics and church dogma, a kind of "purification of the sources."[2] Nicholas of Cusa (1401–1464) developed a monistic method in which God was understood as the unity of the cosmos, knowable through human intelligence. Cusa also explored a comparison of Christianity with Islam and Judaism. Several new German universities became centers of humanism: Heidelberg, Vienna, Leipzig, Munich, and Mainz. Part of the efforts of Christian humanists was directed at the study of the Bible. Johannes Reuchlin (1455–1522) at Heidelberg revived interest in the study of Hebrew language in order to interpret properly the Old Testament. Similarly, Desiderius Erasmus (c.1466–1536), preeminent among the Christian humanists, insisted upon the necessity of knowledge of the natural world, of the rules of rhetoric, and use of the classical poets in order to interpret Scripture rightly. His premier accomplishment, a critical edition of the New Testament (1516), spawned a new venture in the science of textual criticism. John Colet (c.1467–1519) at Oxford developed a literary critical method of interpreting the letters of Paul, while in France Jacques Lefevre d'Etaples (c.1460–1536) used comparative philology to prepare commentaries on the Psalms, the Gospels, and the General Epistles. The Protestant reformers of the sixteenth century, to a person, would be greatly indebted to the humanistic achievements.

Perhaps the symbol of new Reformed approaches to studying Christianity was the German university. As we have seen, the popes chartered the earliest universities in the region and the Church licensed the faculties. In 1527, however, Philip the Magnanimous, the Landgrave of Marburg, deviated from that practice and started the University of Marburg, the first university belonging to the Protestant tradition, and chartered by a civil government. Philip's University, as it came to be called, had faculties in theology, humanities, and the arts. The university set the stage for intense self-criticism of the Christian religious tradition.

In the seventeenth and eighteenth centuries, Enlightenment thinkers unleashed a scathing critique of Christianity, largely as a reaction to perceived clericalism and superstition, as well as claims of miracles and the notion of divine revelation. They variously championed religious toleration and the integration of faith and the sciences. Protestants were committed to Enlightenment principles because the Enlightenment stood against the prevailing Roman Catholic deterministic view of human nature and practice of authoritarian religion. For instance, Francois Turretini devoted student of the teachings of John Calvin, modernized Calvinism by downplaying original sin and predestination. Instead, he preferred the moral aspects of the Reformed faith. Edward Gibbon at the Royal Academy in London made a long-lasting historiographical contribution in his reinterpretation of Roman history in which he expressed his distress at the decline of the greatness of Rome whilst Christianity advanced. This generation of critics, as Peter Gay has quipped, became a cluster of "cuckoos in the Christian nest."[3]

By the later seventeenth century, Christianity and reason were firmly wed in learned circles. The Englishman John Locke became the prince of enlightened Christians, as his work, *The Reasonableness of Christianity* (1695) illustrates; later Mathew Tindal's *Christianity as Old as the Creation* (1730) made a similar case for Christianity as a religion of nature. Likewise, Gotthold E. Lessing, son of a theologian and an influential German poet and philosopher, was interested in the seriousness of theological questions, but not in any of its supernatural claims. In a harsher critique, the Frenchman Voltaire moved far beyond Locke's "reasonable pulpit-style Christianity" to a more personally rewarding religion of nature. The Scottish philosopher, David Hume, wrote of the scandal of miracles in 1737, while the Dutch rationalist Baruch Spinoza labeled Jesus, Moses, and Mohammed "the great imposters." More conservative thinkers, dubbed "neologians" attempted to keep the traditional language of Christianity but gave the words new meanings devoid of supernaturalism. Christian Wolf at Marburg taught that revelation might transcend reason, but never contradict it. Taken collectively, these religious critics or "philosophes" as they were labeled in France made a virtue of questioning and forever after subjected Christianity to close scrutiny.

In the lead of a self-critical Christianity were professional and academic historians, theologians, and biblical scholars lodged firmly in the university faculties. The critical documentary approach of historians like Leopold von Ranke in Germany separated the myths of Christianity from the identifiable historical contexts and events, particularly as applied to the Protestant Reformation. This in turn caused theologians to use principles laid down by G. F. Hegel, like the recovery of dialectical thinking, to distinguish between the Jesus of history and the existential Christ of faith. Hegel's method gave a new strategy to the analysis of Christianity in its historical and political contexts. The early twentieth century was dominated by "Neo-Orthodox" theologians and biblical scholars like Karl Barth, Emil Brunner, and Rudolph Bultmann and existentialist theologians like Paul Tillich who, with a dialectic approach, moved the discourse of Christianity well beyond traditional doctrinal and ecclesial bounds while retaining much of its historic vocabulary. This essentially historicist orientation influentially emanating from Albrect Ritschl at the University of Berlin also produced the groundbreaking sociological approaches to analyzing Christianity by Max Weber at Heidelberg, *The Protestant Ethic and the Spirit of Capitalism* (1904), and Ernst Troeltsch, also at Heidelberg, *The Social Teaching of the Christian Churches* (1911).

As we shall discover in discussing below the missionary character of Christianity, the interaction of Christian missionaries with practitioners of other world religions in the nineteenth century led to a serious study of other religious values and rituals. The result was the emergence of the theological discipline of ecumenics and the pursuit of interfaith or interreligious dialog. A high point in this interaction of Christianity with other religions came in 1893 with the convening of the World's Parliament of Religions. The Parliament, convened in Chicago with the endorsement of its reconstituted university, featured lectures and exhibits by confessing Buddhists, Muslims, Hindus, Sikhs, Jains, Taoists, and Confucianists. In the ensuing decades, Christianity came to be treated as one of the world's major religions, to use the term then in vogue, phenomenologically.

In North American terms, from the early nineteenth century most universities and colleges taught subjects relating to Christian culture, bible, Christian evidences, and ecclesiastical history. Typically, persons trained for pastoral ministry who might have earned a master's degree taught these subjects. Commencing in the 1830s, a modest amount of intellectual ferment was noticeable in the urban institutions, many of which imitated trends in Britain and Germany. The pace quickened with the advent of graduate research schools in the 1870s like Johns Hopkins and the transformations of Harvard and Yale universities. At the forefront of "new" American Christian scholarship, however, was the Chicago School, the collective name for an approach and two generations of scholars associated with the University of Chicago. Behind the leadership of William Rainey Harper, a Semiticist and philologist, an array of specialists like George W. Northrup and Shailer Mathews (theology), Shirley Jackson Case (history), Ernest Dewitt Burton (New Testament), George Burman Foster (philosophy of religion), Albion Small (church and society), and Henry Mabie (world religions) redefined the parameters of the Christian religion according to its evolved values in historical contexts and its commonalties with non-Christian religions. Others like C. H. Toy at Harvard, Jacob G. Schurman at Cornell University, Morton S. Enslin and James Pritchard at the University of Pennsylvania, and William F. Albright at Johns Hopkins University, each contributed to a broadened understanding of Judeao-Christianity as a defining social and political force in Western and Eastern civilizations.

A genuine North American watershed in studying Christianity was the work of H. Richard Niebuhr. His 1929 book, *The Social Sources of Denominationalism*, itself based upon the earlier work of Ernst Troeltsch, Max Weber, R. H. Tawney, and Adolf Harnack, set aside orthodox approaches to understanding the different categories of Christianity (the "denominations"), favoring instead a principle of differentiation that lay in their conformity to the order of social classes and castes.[4] Niebuhr used the language of social construction, the "disinherited," the middle class, immigrants, sectionalism, and nationalism, to classify Catholics, Presbyterians, Anglicans, and Baptists. While numerous later scholars quibbled with his categories, Niebuhr's theoretical construct spawned a cottage industry of scholars and "ecclesiocrats" who translated confessions and structures into choices or aspirations according to socioeconomic factors. Anyone interested in the meaning of Christianity in the United States' and Canadian contexts where religious plurality is the norm, must work through Niebuhrian ideas.

One of the results of a searching self-critical Christian scholarship was the emergence of a robust and assertive evangelical Christianity. The word "evangelical" first came into common usage in the Reformation era when it was the equivalent of "reformed." Later, it came to be synonymous with a pietistic, experiential, biblical form of Christianity in contrast with sacramental or political forms. In the nineteenth century, as mainstream Christian scholarship tended to become overly critical, Evangelicals put their efforts to work in defense of a Christianity that was synchronous with the primitive church and with a vital understanding of the Lordship of Christ. This resulted in a renewed emphasis upon biblical studies to recover the central thought and evidences of the first century, plus the heritage of an unbroken fidelity to transforming discipleship. Evangelicals joined hands with those in Christian mission who looked to world evangelization through preaching, teaching, translation, and caregiving missions. Underpinning their efforts have been solid intellectual accomplishments from biblical scholars like F. W. Gotch, H. Wheeler Robinson, B. F. Westcott, J. F. A. Hort, J. B. Lightfoot, H. H. Rowley, F. F. Bruce, and B. M. Metzger. Among evangelical historians, one finds names like K. S. Latourette, J. Edwin Orr, Justo Gonzales, and more recently Mark Noll. Additionally, Evangelicals are to be found in a wide variety of scholarly endeavors, including, C. S. Lewis and John Stott (apologetics), Helmut Thielicke and Louis Smedes (ethics), David Moberg and Reginald Bibby (sociology), and Clyde Narramore and Wayne Oates (psychology and counseling). In recent decades, Evangelicals have represented a conservative, apologetic form of Christian studies with all the rationalistic urgency of the Enlightenment.

Other special interest groups have plunged deeply into Christian Studies. Beginning in the 1920s, Black scholars began to reinterpret the Christian narrative in terms of slavery and oppression. Booker T. Washington and Marcus Garvey differed on outcomes but agreed on the influence of Christianity upon the African experience. Fostered in the Chicago School orientation were Howard Thurman, Mordecai Johnson, Miles Mark Fisher, and Benjamin Mays. Later powerful exponents of the Black American experience as a liberating and reconciling movement have been Adam Clayton Powell, Jr., Martin Luther King, Jr., James Cone, and J. Deotis Roberts in the United States, and Desmond Tutu and Leon Sullivan in the South African struggle against apartheid. The great contribution of Black theology is that theology must grow out of the context of experience.

Similar to the Black Studies school is the feminist critique of Christianity. Here major writers like Mary Daly, Phyllis Trible, Elisabeth Schussler Fiorenza,

Rosemary Radford Reuther, Mercy Amba, Betty Govinden, and Sallie McFague have severely critiqued traditional Christianity as a form of institutionalized patriarchy. They find hope for Christianity as it breaks away from a male religious orientation, a male-dominant clergy, and gender specific vocabulary, to equity among the sexes, and an entirely new sense of the cosmos that values the feminine. Christianity must address the plight of women worldwide, they collectively argue.

Finally, the Liberationist and postcolonialist interpreters have used the history of Christian thought and a revisionist theology to create new readings of Judaeo-Christian Scripture that unmask imperialist interpretations and empower communities to social and political transformation. For Gustavo Gutierrez in 1988, "Theology [was] critical reflection on praxis in light of the Bible."[5] There is a powerful impulse in Latin American liberation theology toward freedom. With respect to African Christianity, Lamin Sanneh in his seminal book, *Translating the Message: The Missionary Impact on Culture* (1989), has suggested that the full brunt of colonialism has been lessened by the translation of the Judeo-Christian Scriptures into indigenous African languages, thus giving rise to a rich variety of African Christian subcultures.

A scathing critique of Christianity emerged from within Christianity itself in the 1950s and 1960s. The voices of key Neo-Orthodox theologians at mid-century were replaced by a new generation of thinkers who were asking genuinely "radical" questions. Important books appeared such as Paul Van Buren's *The Secular Meaning of the Gospel* (1963), William Hamilton's *Radical Theology and the Death of God* (1963), and Harvey Cox's *The Secular City* (1965). In an explosive era politically focused primarily upon the United States and its foreign policy, theology became a means of political commentary: the consensus was that the traditional forms and vocabulary of Christian thought were found wanting. The new focus came to be on the actual finite world in which humans lived, not the idealism of the longstanding Christian institution, nor any beatific vision of eternal life. Prompted by a secular existentialist philosopher Martin Heidegger at the University of Marburg, and moved ahead by a new breed of Christian theologians, Jürgen Moltmann, Johannes Metz, and Roger Garaudy, a conversation opened between Christianity and Marxism. This conversation produced at least three results: a useful catharsis for both Marxism and Christianity; a new understanding of Christianity in Socialist countries; and a new integrity among Christians to ask any question and seek the most radical alternatives: secular, revolutionary, or primitivist. The Christian-Marxist dialog opened the door for Christian engagement with Black, Brown, Red, and Yellow races and the need for a more universal ethic and understanding of transcendence. Inevitably, the liberationist, feminist, and postmodern critics took up the opportunity, nurtured along by the social sciences.

Lately, the social sciences have again opened new approaches to the study of Christianity, and vice versa. A foundational classic that integrated psychology and historical biography was Erik Erikson's *Young Man Luther* (1949). Erikson concluded that Luther bore all the marks of an abused child with a lifelong gastrointestinal difficulty and that his "evangelical breakthrough" occurred in the toilet, not in the study. Later psychohistorians like Lloyd de Mause have drawn Christian religious factors into their analysis of contemporary world figures. The well-known American sociologist, Rodney Stark, has ventured into early Christian development of the first five centuries CE, and using demographic and social group identification methods, has offered persuasive revisionist interpretations of the role of women in the movement, the transition from Judaism, and the class structure of emerging Christians. Recent anthropologists like William Hurlburt and theologians like Philip Hefner are looking into the question of what it means to be human and the theological relevance of new areas of inquiry like sociobiology. Some Christian theologians are quite intrigued with the work of anthropologists like Ward Goodenough and Solomon Katz who suggest that primitive peoples have a human capacity for belief or that changes in religion may have prompted the transition to agriculture in premodern societies. An exceptionally useful example of a holistic social science approach to human civilization, including Christian religious cultures, is Jared Diamond's *Guns, Germs, and Steel: The Fates of Human Societies* (1997; 2003). To be completely balanced, however, John Millank, a Christian theologian at Cambridge University, has insightfully challenged the assumptions and results of a social theory critique of religion as in fact a disguised form of theology that promotes a certain secular consensus. Millbank boldly urges that the sociology of religion ought to come to an end![6]

Political scientists, public policy analysts, social workers, futurologists, geographers, and demographers have all become accustomed to Christian categories and sets of data that identify public attitudes, voting trends, legislative initiatives, and socioeconomic projections. Having commenced in the United States and Canada, and at the London School of Economics, this type of data gathering and interpretation influences decisions about the environment, stem cell research, pandemic diseases, militarism, and political ideologies in places as far-flung as Latin America, Ireland, Russia, equatorial

Africa, South Africa, and the nations of the Pacific Rim. Among the leading interpreters of data with a quasi-Christian perspective are the Heritage Foundation, the Brookings Institute, the Pew Research Center, and the Gallup Organization and writers like David Barrett, an internationally recognized religious demographer. Various Christian media outlets make use of the work of Alvin Tofler (*Future Shock*), John Naisbitt (*Megatrends*), Peter Drucker (*Men, Ideas, and Politics*), Stephen Hawking (*A Brief History of Time*), and Richard John Neuhaus (*First Things*).

Theological inquiry has also changed profoundly. Christian "Process" theologians following the lead of Alfred North Whitehead (1861–1947), have offered intriguing alternatives to traditional classical Christian theism. Theologians like Henry N. Wieman, Charles Hartshorne, John Cobb, and Shubert Ogden have redefined God from being thought of as a cosmic moralist or controlling power to "creative-responsive love" who acts creatively in the world primarily by persuasion. By empirical observation, these thinkers posit evil and calamity in the world, suggest that these realities are part of the working out of God's allowance of human freedom, and are not incompatible with God's beneficence toward all his creatures. The traditional theistic position of the sovereignty of God becomes in process thought only a last resort.[7] Process thought has opened new bridges between Christians and other world religions and by embracing evolutionary science, its advocates have engaged a new kind of conversation with scientists who are interested in existential concerns. A vast new array of thinkers is involved in dialog about Christian religious issues and communities: for instance, Michael Benedikt at the University of Texas has resuscitated the "Argument from Design" from an architectural perspective, and classicists and archaeologists are unearthing artifacts that demonstrate social and cultural transformation pointing toward the Christianization of Classical Civilization.

Scientific inquiry has been both advanced and retarded by Christian culture. At the beginning of the fifth century, St. Augustine rejected the power of astronomy to predict person's lives, favoring instead divine revelation in the Scriptures. The papacy would easily follow Augustine's lead in establishing an authority for the Church over all learning. As we have seen, the Renaissance opened up inquiry in the humanities that led to new theories of a scientific kind. While the Church condemned anatomical and physiological experimentation, Christian scientists forged ahead like Michael Servetus (1511–1553) with a study and later a description of pulmonary circulation. He was burned at the stake in Geneva for questioning the doctrine of the trinity. In the next century, Galileo Gallilei (1564–1642) was condemned to house arrest for life in 1633 for promoting a Copernican idea of the universe. That ban was only lifted in 1978 by Pope John Paul II. Little wonder why a significant movement among philosophers and scientists, beginning with Auguste Comte (1798–1857), set aside the "theological era" in which persons depended upon the church and overarching metaphysical principles in favor of a "scientific age" in which only that which can be verified by observation and finite, cognitively meaningful procedures is valid. As "logical positivists" who believed in the cumulative results of science, they created a lively debate with Christian thinkers.

Withal, there remains a long-term preoccupation among Christians who are scientists with the processes and timing/duration of planet earth's origins. On the one hand, there are persons of faith who want to accept the fruits of scientific discovery, which inevitably suggests that the earth is very old and has undergone several eras of cataclysmic change, thus accommodating the age of the dinosaurs and the ice epochs. On the other hand, there are critical believers who are persuaded that science is faulty in its methods and when inquiry runs counter to a literal reading of Scripture, revelation trumps science. In contemporary circles, there are mathematicians, physicists, and philosophers who are Christians, like William Dembski and John Polkinghorne who teach "intelligent design," whereby they assert that there is a high probability that biological structures were assembled by a nonnatural agent, which in turn leads to a theistic position. And, there is a substantial school of biblical "inerrantist" Christians who subscribe to the "Creationist" interpretation of the origins of the universe whereby the descriptions in Genesis 1–2 are taken literally. Generally, Creationists are disinclined toward the theory of evolution because it reduces the role of a sovereign creator and independently created species. Flowing from a traditional Christian theological understanding of Creation, Christian philosophers and theologians interact with medical scientists and biologists on questions relating to eugenics, genetic engineering, definitions of the beginning and ending of life, and life beyond death.

Beyond the Christian interest in cosmology, there is a steady conversation between Christianity and science in other areas. For instance, advocates of artificial intelligence raise the issue of rights for robots, and conversely, of whether humans are basically a type of machine. Routine questions among Christians arise over the ethics of organ transplants, the understanding of dreams, factors determining human behavior, and the possibility of extraterrestrial life in the distant galaxies. Francis Collins, longtime head of the Human Genome Project, is both a Creationist for Christian religious reasons and an advocate of the evolutionary hypothesis for scientific purposes.

The student approaching Christianity will find a multifarious religious tradition, one that is historic, adaptable, self-critical, and unified across time and context in its essentials, yet very diverse in its applications. One must be careful to recognize that the global Christian religious community is generally delineated between Roman Catholics (1.1 billion), Protestants (550 million), Pentecostals (480 million), Evangelicals (420 million), and Orthodox (225 million). Each of these categories brings a unique theological and cultural orientation to the meaning of Christianity. What unites these divergent strands of over two billion Christians is the central figure of Jesus Christ historically and theologically, and various channels of ecumenical dialog and infrequent areas of mission and cooperation.

For further reading and study

Clifford, Anne M. *Introducing Feminist Theology*. Maryknoll, NY: Orbis Books, 2002.

Cobb, John B., and Griffin, David Ray. *Process Theology: An Introductory Exposition*. Louisville, KY: Westminster John Know Press, 1976.

Cone, James H. *God of the Oppressed*. New York: Seabury Press, 1975.

Cupitt, Don. *Reforming Christianity*. Santa Rosa, CA: Polebridge Press, 2001.

Dean, Thomas. *Post-Theistic Thinking: The Marxist-Christian Dialogue in Radical Perspective*. Philadelphia, PA: Temple University Press, 1975.

Diamond, Jared. *Guns, Germs, and Steel: The Fates of Human Societies*. New York: W.W. Norton, 1997.

Encyclopedia of Science and Religion, 2 vols. Edited by J. Wenzel Vrede van Huyssteen. New York: Macmillan Reference, 2003.

Gay, Peter. *The Enlightenment: An Interpretation: The Rise of Modern Paganism*. London: Weidenfeld and Nicolson, 1966.

Gutierrez, Gustavo. *Theology of Liberation: History, Politics, and Salvation*. Maryknoll, NY: Orbis Books, 1988.

Niebuhr, Richard H. *The Social Sources of Denominationalism*. New York: Henry Holt and Company, 1929.

Millbank, John. *Theology and Social Theory: Beyond Secular Reason*. Oxford: Blackwell, 1990.

Rowland, Christopher, editor. *The Cambridge Companion to Liberation Theology*. Cambridge: Cambridge University Press, 1999.

Stark, Rodney. *The Rise of Christianity: A Sociologist Reconsiders History*. Princeton, NJ: Princeton University Press, 1996.

Troeltsch, Ernst. *The Social Teachings of the Christian Churches*. London: George Allen and Unwin, 1911.

1 Foundations and Scripture

Our quest to understand the Christian tradition begins at the beginning. Jesus of Nazareth is the founder of Christianity. In this respect, he compares in the narrative with Gautama, Mohammed, Mahavira, Nanak, Abraham, and Confucius. In terms of sheer historicity, more is knowable about Jesus than many other "founders" of religious traditions. Beyond history, however, for Christians, Jesus is also the Son of God and thus his place in the Christian religion is of inestimable religious importance. Christians consider Jesus unique. What we know of Jesus, and how we know, are of fundamental importance to establishing the claims of Christianity. It is stating the obvious to observe that the name of the religious tradition is derived from Jesus Christ, a practice first noticed in Antioch of Syria in the first century. In this chapter, we shall examine the sources of information about Jesus, the basic story line of Jesus, the theological significance Christians attach to Jesus, and how his life continues to shape Christianity. We shall also look into the life and work of Paul who led the second generation of the Christian tradition and became the most important interpreter of the life and work of Jesus.

Christians and the Hebrew Scriptures

The Christian tradition is built upon Jewish history and religious culture. It is widely held among Christian interpreters that the full meaning of the Hebrew Scriptures is to be found in Jesus Christ, the Messiah of God. In fact, Christians refer to the Hebrew canon as the "Old Testament" or ancient covenant held in narrative tandem with the New Testament or "covenant of the Lord Jesus Christ."

As we shall see, Jesus was schooled in the scriptures of the Jewish religion and he highlighted on many occasions his acceptance of the law and the prophets, and his own role in the fulfillment of ancient prophecies. Often, he quoted the Hebrew Scriptures, though it is widely held that he was likely familiar with the Septuagintal Greek version of the books.[1] At one point, he indicated that he had come to fulfill the law and the prophets, not to destroy them,[2] and in the last moments of his crucifixion he recalled words of the Psalmist, "My God, my God, why have you forsaken me?"[3] To make the connection with the narratives of Israel to the stories of Jesus, Christian interpreters, since the early church, have seen theophanies in the Old Testament that they believe reveal Jesus in a pre-incarnational[4] mode and, especially when interpreting prophetic and apocalyptic passages, Christian teachings place a meaning upon futuristic details that reach far beyond the restoration of Jews to Israel or Israel's political kingdoms before the Common Era. A noted nonconformist preacher of the nineteenth century claimed that he could follow a scarlet thread through the entire Old and New Testaments, finding on every page some aspect of Christ. It is more than accurate to categorize Christianity as an Abrahamic faith, by which one means that it shares the heritage of the Jewish people from the time of the Patriarchs and the Islamic faith from the offspring of Ishmael. As one writer has put it, the Old Testament is such a critically important work that "apart from it both Christendom and western culture would be inconceivable."[5]

The sources about Jesus

Christian scholarship has spent a good deal of time and effort on the question of what is to be known about Jesus and the sources pertaining to his life and work. Most New Testament scholars agree that there were four stages of development in telling the story of Jesus.[6] First, there were those who were eyewitnesses to his work during his lifetime. Jesus could write, as suggested in John 8.6, 8, but he left no records himself. More significantly, as far as anyone knows, there are no surviving written records from the period of his lifetime. This includes any public records or historical data from any Roman or Palestinian source. Some have speculated that there may have been Jewish sources, but these were doubtlessly lost when the City of Jerusalem and the Temple were destroyed in 70 CE. Second, from about 30 CE to at least 50 CE and maybe as late as 90 CE, the details of Jesus were basically in an oral form as a story, a parable, or a model prayer. The writer of the Gospel of Luke tells his readers that he was collecting and ordering such material (Luke 1.2). A third stage evolved from about 50 CE to 70 CE as written sources began to appear among the Christian assemblies. These materials were likely letters from leaders like Paul, plus fragments of the beginnings of the gospels, like Mark, which may be dated as early as the fifties. Finally, there was the ultimate work of the evangelists, the writers and compilers of Mark, Matthew, Luke, and John (plus later gospel writers), who deliberately created the authoritative accounts that the churches used widely and preserved. Christians hold that during this time of development of a literary corpus, the Holy Spirit was at work in the community inspiring writers and guiding the versions toward a consensus about Jesus.

We must now turn to the texts themselves that tell the stories of Jesus. They are called "gospels" from the Greek term, *euangellios* that means "good news." A "gospel" is a particular kind of biographical literature. More than just an historical sketch, a gospel is woven around a central character and follows a theological theme. Luke wrote his gospel as a serious example of history/biography and his main theme was to present Jesus as the Savior of the world. John tells his readers that his bias was that his readers might "believe that Jesus is the Christ, the Son of God; and that believing they might have life through his name."[7] Apparently, the writer of Matthew wanted to impress his readers with the point that Jesus was the Messiah of Israel, fulfilling prophecy and carefully detailed in the genealogies. Mark, the earliest gospel, began his story by asserting that Jesus was the Son of God.

During the period from about 50 CE to 150 CE, a written tradition was emerging about the life of Jesus along with interpretations of the Christian message as Paul, John, Peter, and others taught it. Some Christians believe that the basic teachings about Jesus were given to the churches by a special work of the Holy Spirit, who inspired certain writers to give a faithful and authoritative account. Others believe that there were clearly differing traditions about Jesus that contended for supremacy. Gradually, according to this approach, a "proto-orthodox" tradition emerged that sought to recover and continue what the original disciples of Jesus had heard and taught. Whatever the pathway, by the middle of the fourth century, the Church had agreed upon a "canon" or sacred body of authoritative scriptures. Most recognize the list that Athanasius, the influential bishop of Alexandria, Egypt, compiled in 367 CE a list establishing the authoritative canon, which he called the "New Testament." At the heart of this body of literature was the life of Jesus. As far as manuscripts of these biographical and interpretive accounts are concerned, the oldest thus far is a section of the Gospel of John, dated about 125 CE. The earliest complete copies of the gospels date from 200 CE and there are widely divergent readings for several passages. For instance, the Gospel of Mark contains no less than four distinct endings, all dating from before 500, and a majority of scholars believe the fourth chapter of John is a later addition to the rest of that gospel. The advanced student of Christianity is thus left to decide which collection of inspired textual variants constitutes an authoritative text for investigation.

The life of Jesus

Christians have always been preoccupied with the life of Jesus. As early as the later first century after the life of Jesus, various attempts were made to harmonize the existing accounts into a single life of Jesus. Tatian (c.110–120), a Mesopotamian convert, was among those who took this approach. Later, during the Middle Ages, legends and traditions from beyond the Scriptures were added to the material in the gospels. The role of Mary, for instance, was expanded to account for Jesus' supernatural birth; this image was drawn from the *Gospel of James* (early second century) and lent credence to mediaeval ideas like the "Blessed Virgin" Mary and Mary as the "Mother of God."

It was during the Renaissance that humanist scholars in Europe like Erasmus followed a more historical path in understanding the life of Jesus, attempting to locate the best manuscripts and strip away the added materials from the Middle Ages. Rationalists in the Age of Enlightenment were often radical in their attempts to separate the man Jesus from all of the theological claims. Many writers denied the occurrence of miraculous and mysterious events in Jesus' ministry, like John Toland's work, *Christianity Not Mysterious*

(1696). Beginning in the late eighteenth century with H. S. Reimarus, a linguist in Hamburg, Germany, recovery of the life of Jesus became a major scholarly pursuit. Reimarus held that Jesus' disciples had re-created the image of Jesus from what was essentially a failed religious mission. In the 1830s David F. Strauss brought forth his life of Jesus in which he claimed that most of the Jesus stories were myths and much of the material in the New Testament could not be understood as historical. Much criticism came upon Strauss for his radical assertions, yet the questions remained. At the turn of the twentieth century, Albert Schweitzer, biblical scholar, missionary, and musician, offered his "quest for the historical Jesus" in which he allowed that the church had a profound influence upon what can be known of Jesus and that eschatology (a study of last things) had a significant role to play in understanding Jesus' teachings. William Wrede, a contemporary of Schweitzer, pursued the "messianic secret" of Mark's gospel and concluded that it was basically a literary device. In the train of Schweitzer and Wrede came Rudolf Bultmann and Karl Barth. Both of these writers, influenced by the Marburg professor, Wilhelm Hermann, emphasized an existential Christ over the historical figure Jesus. Bultmann tied the relevance of Christianity not to objective details, but to 'existential' truth, and Barth chose to underscore the importance of Christ as the Word of God. Paul Tillich, a leading philosophical theologian of the next generation, even went so far as to claim that historical criticism could come to the judgment that the man Jesus of Nazareth never lived and Tillich thus held that details of Jesus' life were not of decisive importance.[8]

In recent New Testament scholarship, however, a new "quest" began in the mid-twentieth century. Following upon methods introduced by Bultmann and Hermann Gunkel labeled "form criticism,"[9] Gunther Bornkamm of the University of Heidelberg, inaugurated a search for the real Jesus in his book, *Jesus of Nazareth* (1960) that sought to take the details of Jesus' life seriously. Bornkamm and others emphasized the importance of a "kerygma"[10] or central core teaching about Jesus that lies at the heart of all the gospels. With Willi Marxsen and Hans Conzelmann, Bornkamm used a method called "redaction criticism" to gain insights into the work of compilers of the gospels in creating the traditions about Jesus. Wolfhart Pannenburg, theology professor at Munich, has likewise built upon Bornkamm's work in reasserting the historicity of the gospel accounts. More recently, the "Jesus Seminar," convened in 1985 by Robert Funk in Berkeley, California, employed major New Testament scholars in a project to ascertain which of the sayings of Jesus in the New Testament actually belonged to him.[11] Bruce Malina and others have pursued a social scientific approach to the backgrounds of Jesus' life. Raymond E. Brown and David Aune together represent those scholars who use a literary–historical analysis. In the last two decades, approaches that are ever more radical have emerged in New Testament studies, including deconstructionism and postcolonialism. Deconstructionists follow the lead of literary critics like Jacques Derrida and want to know what is hidden or derived in an ordinary reading of a text. The goal of critics like David Seeley and Ellen Armour, for instance, is not to reach some sort of decisive conclusion or valid information about Jesus. Rather, deconstructionists argue that reading the life of Jesus has more to do with a reader's interests than with a text. Postcolonialists like Fernando Segovia and R. S. Sugirtharajah want to break away from colonial and imperialistic readings of Jesus' life and relate his teachings to a more globalized religious community. What is evident in the history of Jesus scholarship is that there continues to be a fascination with details of his life and the Christian community is sufficiently tolerant to allow even radical self-criticism of one whom they claim to be God's Son.

The story line of Jesus

If one conflates the events recorded in the four gospels into a single account, a chronologically reasonable sequence of events emerges. The major pivotal events in the life of Jesus fall into the following categories: infancy and the early years; the baptism and Galilean ministry; accounts of Jesus' ministry in Judea and Perea; the final days in Jerusalem or the Passion Period.

The infancy details of Jesus' life are contextualized by references to the reign of Caesar Augustus, King Herod, and a "governor" in Syria named Quirinius. Associated with these historical personages were a census that was said to be the cause of Joseph and Mary's return to Bethlehem, and some sort of celestial occurrence, most likely a lunar eclipse or a planetary confluence. Most scholars agree the details suggest a date of 6–4 BCE for Jesus' birth. The main characters in the infancy stories are Mary, a young unmarried Jewish woman of Nazareth who found herself pregnant, and Joseph, a Jewish man who also resided in Nazareth in Galilee, but who was originally from Bethlehem and belonged to the tribe of Judah. Secondary characters include Mary's cousin, Elizabeth, and her husband Zacharias, who lived near Jerusalem where he was a priest at the Temple. Elizabeth and Zacharias, both advanced in years, were the parents of John the Baptizer, a cousin to Jesus and a kind of prophetic advance spokesman for the work of Jesus. Since neither Mark nor John provide any details about Jesus' parentage, it may be assumed that the early churches were hungry for such details and the gospels of Luke and Matthew met those needs.

Matthew's account largely passes over the birth scene, preferring to justify Joseph's acceptance of a pregnant woman as his wife. This would have been important to a Jewish Christian readership and it helps to ratify the unique purpose of Matthew's gospel. It is in Luke's narrative that we learn that there was an arduous journey from northern Israel (the region of Galilee) to the south (Judea), where the couple found no lodging for Mary as she prepared to give birth. Mary gave birth to Jesus in a stable, taking care of the child's needs as lovingly as a young mother would be expected to. The rather mundane accounts are greatly enhanced by supernatural phenomena: angelic announcements to Mary and Joseph, declaring the nature of the anticipated birth; an angelic presence near Bethlehem, singing in the heavens; an angelic announcement to nearby shepherds; a bright star that seems to hover over the birth site; and another angelic revelation to Joseph about the child's welfare. Matthew added a post-birth story of the visitation of eastern astrologers/dignitaries who bring gifts to the child whom they assumed had a special, royal status. Like any Jewish child of the era, Jesus was circumcised and presented in the Temple at Jerusalem. Matthew's account again added new details in the saga of Joseph's family having to flee to Egypt to avoid the edict of King Herod to execute all newborn children as potential threats to his throne. The "infancy" narratives in the four gospels conclude with an annual Passover Feast visit of Joseph's family again to Jerusalem where twelve-year-old Jesus is found in the Temple in dialog with the teachers.

The foregoing outline is what the majority of the Christian community has accepted as the reliable details of the early life of Jesus of Nazareth. There has long been an assumption that many of the infancy details in Luke's narrative may have originated with Mary, the mother of Jesus, because of the affectionate particulars of childcare. However, as early as the late first century, there were other "gospel" attempts to supply details of Jesus' early life, particularly the "silent" years of his childhood and adolescence. In the *Infancy Gospel of Thomas* (c.125 CE), for instance, the child Jesus performed miracles that become misadventures and he came under discipline by his father, Joseph. He eventually came to use his powers for good, according to this tradition. In the *Gospel of James*, the miraculous character of Jesus' mother, Mary, is stressed. Details are given such as Mary's continued relations with Joseph and a postpartum examination. Scholars of the contemporary era consider these "other gospels" important because there was a clearly established group or emerging "canon" of gospels that the mainstream of Christians recognized, rejecting less antique versions, and yet they exhibit a widespread interest in the life and teachings of Jesus.[12]

The next stage of the stories of Jesus commenced with his baptism. The baptism of Jesus is a relevant detail in his biography for several reasons. First, the rite of baptism (discussed in Chapter 4) recalls an ancient initiatory and purification rite still in contemporary use among sects like the Essenes. An intriguing question that remains is whether John the Baptizer, who baptized his cousin Jesus, received the practice from the Essenes. Second, the baptism of Jesus, according to Matthew's and John's gospels, became the point of beginning and certification of his ministry. The gospel writers add details to the ritual that indicate a voice from heaven, words of pleasure from Jesus' Heavenly Father, and the presence of a dove which Luke, Matthew, and John call the Holy Spirit. This event thus became an authority for Jesus as well as a basis for understanding his sacral commission later in the story.

Matthew, Mark, and Luke next include a story called the temptation of Jesus. From the high moment of his baptism, Jesus is led into the "wilderness" to be tested by the devil [Satan]. The testing lasts for 40 days during which Jesus ate nothing and became famished. He entered into a dialog with the devil who offered him first, food and then political authority. The ultimate test was of Jesus' divine powers to save himself from a precipitous fall. Jesus heroically passed all three tests and denounced the devil as an imposter. Thus, Jesus' ministry continued to be ratified.

The four canonical gospels now take an approach to the life of Jesus in a chronological extent of about 3 years. One of the first tasks that Jesus undertook was the assemblage of a comradeship, referred to as his disciples or followers. Below we shall discuss how this group became a nexus of the church; here the disciples will be presented as Jesus' students. They were from various parts of Galilee, from a wide variety of occupations, and from time to time increased and decreased in number. Some, as Peter and Andrew, James and John, were fishermen; others included a tax collector, a laborer, and a person engaged in financial matters. There were women in Jesus' close following, though the gospel writers were careful not to list them along with the disciples in any formal way. Having made the choices of his associates, they and Jesus begin to itinerate around Galilee on what is referred to as the "great Galilean mission."

Accounts of the Galilean mission reckon that it occurred between summer/ autumn 27 CE to Spring of 29 CE.[13] Several aspects of this period of Jesus' ministry are noteworthy. First, he had difficulty in his hometown of Nazareth.

In the local synagogue, he associated himself with the prophecy of Isaiah, only to raise the wrath of those who heard him. They rejected him because of his family background and ultimately ran him out of the city. He went to Capernaum, a village on the shore of the Sea of Galilee and set up a base there with a more congenial reception. Second, Jesus' reputation as a healer of sick people gained much momentum in Galilee. He is seen as casting out demonic spirits, healing the mother-in-law of his new disciple, Peter, and numerous others, lepers, paralytics, and lamed persons. In a momentary display of his supernatural powers, Jesus appeared at a wedding in the village of Cana where with his mother present, he transformed water into wine and resupplied the wedding feast. Apparently, Jesus made regular forays to Jerusalem, as had his parents, to attend the Passover Feasts. The Gospel of John recalls a scene in Jerusalem when he was involved in an altercation in the Temple over the use of sacred space for commercial purposes, which was later to suggest a metaphor of his own death and resurrection.[14]

The Sea of Galilee and its immediate environment became the focal point of Jesus' ministry. On a hillside outside Capernaum he delivered his Sermon on the Mount, arguably one of the greatest rhetorical statement ever recorded. He visited out-of-the-way places and met spiritual opposition, as in Gadara, the home of several psychotic persons. He fished with his disciples on the Sea and used at least one of those occasions to demonstrate his supernatural capacities to walk on water. He denounced the entire nearby cities, Tyre and Sidon, for their moral wickedness. He drew great crowds that frustrated his followers as they had insufficient food supplies and became weary in crowd management. Rather than returning to the villages, Jesus apparently spent time in the mountains north of the Sea of Galilee, for tradition has it that it was on Mt. Hermon that he was "transfigured" with apparitions of Moses and Elijah, again attesting to his divine personage.

A major effort in Jesus' ministry was the training of his inner circle of disciples. Through parables and narratives, he focused upon the Kingdom of God by which he meant the rule of God in human life. The qualities that Jesus stressed included simplicity of religious values, servant-hood, and forgiveness. At times, he spoke of the kingdom as a nearly present reality that he was announcing and inaugurating. At other times, it seemed that the Kingdom was eschatological, that is to be realized in the very distant future. And in still other instances, he spoke of it to Pontius Pilate as "not of this world."[15] According to accounts in Mark's and John's gospels, Jesus declined to conform to popular messianic expectations, which for some was sufficient reason to leave his following.[16] During this period, one learns much about

Jesus' orientation to the Jewish teachings of his day, as he interacted repeatedly with various sects, notably the Scribes, Pharisees, and Sadducees.

Interpreters of Jesus' life cobble together other episodes in his three-year mission around visits he made to Samaria, Perea, and Judea. Samaria, was, of course, off limits for Galileans for racial/ethnic and political reasons, yet Jesus traveled through Samaria on several occasions. To the Gospel of John is appended a fascinating story of Jesus' encounter in Sychar with a Samaritan woman at Jacob's Well, in which he spoke to the religious issues separating contemporary Jews and Samaritans. He also told a story about a "good" Samaritan who assisted a distressed traveler en route to Judea, and he cleansed lepers while passing through Samaria. In 28 or 29 CE Jesus was in Judea for the Feast of Tabernacles and he was confronted by Pharisees about his claims to be the Messiah. A distinct division of opinion arose about him at that time, with Pharisees organizing intense opposition to him, even threatening to stone him. It was in Judea that Jesus appointed additional disciples, 70 in number, to canvass the region. Their efforts, which included miracles and preaching, were overwhelmingly successful. During a visit in Bethany he renewed his friendship with Judean friends Mary, Martha, and Lazarus. On an excursion from Judea, Jesus visited Perea (present-day Jordan) and preached, taught, and healed sick persons there.

The year 30 CE became critical in the life of Jesus of Nazareth. En route to Jerusalem to celebrate the Springtime Feast of the Passover, Jesus entered the final phase of his mission and the climax of all the gospels comes during this period called "his passion." St. Mark's order of the events of Holy Week remained the standard: the triumphal entry into Jerusalem (Palm Sunday), leisure time with friends in Bethany, challenges to Jesus' authority as a teacher, a major discourse on the Mount of Olives, the Last Supper with his disciples in a rented room, the agonizing prayer time in the Garden of Gethsemane, followed by his betrayal, his interrogations and trial(s), the crucifixion, and burial on Friday. The vast majority of orthodox Christians hold that on the third day after his death on the cross, Jesus was resurrected from the dead.[17] By this, it is meant that he was restored to life but his physical body was transformed to a recognizable but spiritual body made of a different substance. The contemporary evidence for the resurrection includes an empty tomb and used but folded grave clothes, supernatural occurrences at his tomb, and postresurrection stories of Jesus appearing to his disciples and publicly for up to 40 days. About a month after the Passion Week, Jesus was together with his followers on the Mount of Olives facing Jerusalem where he gave a final commission to his disciples and was seen to ascend into the heavens. Reports of his appearances continued into the future, for instance to Stephen in Jerusalem, Saul of Tarsus on the road to Damascus, John on Patmos Island, and across the centuries to various Christian persons.

Geopolitically, Jesus' life was contained in a region of approximately 100 miles from north to south and about 50 miles east to west. He lived in the Roman client state called the Kingdom of Herod, and there is no claim that he was a Roman citizen. He acknowledged the political rule of Herod as well as the imperial authority of Caesar. Most scholars believe Jesus was multilingual, having Aramaic as his first language, with a reading knowledge of possibly biblical Hebrew and likely Septuagintal Greek as well. Socially, he had no wife and no offspring. His first home was in Nazareth, later he identified with Capernaum, and he had close acquaintances in Bethany and Jerusalem. His immediate relatives included his mother, Mary, and brothers and sisters. His stepfather, Joseph, is not seen in the canonical gospels after Jesus' visit to Jerusalem at age 12.[18]

A theological understanding of the life of Jesus

For Christians, Jesus' life becomes more than a biased biography. It is the core of their understanding of God. As the various creeds, Nicene, Athanasian, and Apostles' declare, Jesus is fully human and fully divine. Thus, his earthly life had the meaning of ratifying his humanity. The details in history of Jesus' life and ministry are of great importance in underpinning his role in history. During his life, Jesus was born of a woman, grew to adulthood in a family, and had a social and economic life as others of his generation. The gospels are clear that in every respect he was human. Later generations of Christian theologians would debate how his humanity worked out in terms of his will, emotions, nature, and capacity.

In the course of Jesus' human life of approximately 33 years, there were breakthroughs of his divine self. These came at his birth, his baptism, his transfiguration, and his crucifixion and resurrection. These events involved supra-human aspects that Jesus and others attributed to his being divine as well as human. Later, the Church saw in Jesus an eternality that predated his human life and continued thereafter as the Risen or Ascended Lord. This data underscored his divine nature which early theologians called the "hypostatic union." The question of limitations upon Jesus' divine nature due to his life in a human body remained perplexing for many early Christian thinkers.

This duality of Christ's nature provides for human salvation, the first theme in understanding the meaning of the life of Jesus. Unique among all the major religions, in Christian theology God has identified fully with humanity by becoming human as Jesus of Nazareth. This "kenosis" or emptying of himself was voluntary and in no way led to a lessening of his divine character.[19] As Jesus said to his disciple, Phillip, "Whoever has seen me, has seen the Father . . . Believe me that I am in the Father and the Father is in me."[20] God was thus able to redeem humanity through Jesus, to be reconciled to humanity through Jesus, and to see humanity, though sinful, as perfected in Jesus. It is not surprising, therefore, that in the course of fully understanding the meaning and purpose of Jesus, the Church has used paradoxical, contra-dictory assertions about his dual nature and has engaged in linguistic redundancies[21] to state clearly the theological understanding of Jesus.

A second theological theme that is embodied in the life of Jesus is the reign of God, or the kingdom of God. This kingdom was not political or geo-graphical, but a matter of God's sovereignty and authority. Jesus' parables and healings pertain basically to this theme and he is both the herald of the kingdom and the embodiment of its character and principles. The kingdom associated with Jesus contains certain paradoxical elements. At one point, for instance, Jesus spoke of the kingdom as "close at hand."[22] Scholars—and his disciples—have debated whether Jesus thought the kingdom would be estab-lished as a result of his mission. There are also passages in which Jesus taught the kingdom was future, perhaps at a final judgment and the consummation of all things. This may be implied in Jesus' prayer that the "kingdom would come" eventually, as in the parable of the long journey (Luke 19.11–27). Another paradox lies in the connection of the kingdom with Israel's aspirations or with a more universal application. In Mark 13.14ff, Jesus connected the coming kingdom with the prophecy of Daniel and later writers in the Johannine community connected the kingdom with a literal 1,000-year reign of Christ in Israel.[23] The whole point of Luke's version of Jesus' life is that the good news of salvation is offered to all. Paul picked up this theme as well when he turned from being rejected by the Jews to preaching to the Gentiles. In this regard, one must not miss the words of Jesus to the Pharisees, "behold, the kingdom of God is in your midst,"[24] a seeming equation with himself. Even the most radical critics of traditional Christianity agree that the key to under-standing what Jesus was all about was "kingdom religion."[25]

To return to the themes of the four canonical gospels which formed the "kerygma" or original theological understanding of Jesus of Nazareth, one sees what the churches deliberately reinforced in the first century. St. Mark painted a picture of Jesus as a suffering Son of God. This theme is revealed in Jesus' words, "Then he began teaching them that the Son of Man must undergo great suffering . . ."[26] Matthew portrayed Jesus as the fulfillment of the Jewish Messiah (Christ), thus connecting with the fullness of Jewish prophecy and apocalyptic teaching. The opening words of St. Matthew read, "An account of the genealogy of Jesus the Messiah, the son of David, the son of Abraham."[27] Luke went beyond Palestinian and Jewish bounds by seeing Jesus as the savior of the world: "repentance and forgiveness of sins is to be proclaimed in his name to all nations, beginning from Jerusalem."[28] And ultimately, John's gospel taught that Jesus was the Son of Man sent from heaven. In Jesus' prayer for his disciples, he recalled, "Righteous Father, the world does not know you, but I know you; and these know that you have sent me."[29]

What Jesus means to contemporary Christianity

For most Christians, there are two aspects in which the doctrine of Christ, or Christology, matters to the present tradition. Here we must make a distinction between the Jesus of historical accounts and the Risen Lord of Christianity. First, there is the affirmation of the work of God in Christ as it relates to salvation and the purposes of God. Second, Christians hold tenaciously to the belief that Christ is among his people, the Church. This can be in a sacramental way or in a spiritual presence.

The doctrine of salvation cannot be separated from Christology. Jesus' death is understood by Christians to be a sacrifice to provide for their salvation. Roman Catholic Christians hold that the sacrifice of Christ is continual, that is in Jesus' institution of the breaking of the bread and the pouring of the wine in the memorial Supper, a non-bloody continual alternative to his sacrificial death on the cross is made available to Christians to expiate their sins. Many Protestants, however, understand the sacrifice of Christ as "once for all" and finished. All future forgiveness of sins is accomplished by the historic, comprehensive act of Christ on the cross. Christ's work in inviting persons to accept God's gift, in interceding for the needs of his followers before God, and in being a sovereign over all of creation, is accomplished from his ascended position at the right hand of God. So, as the Epistle to the Hebrews declares, the Risen Lord resides in heaven: "We have a high priest who is seated on the right hand of the throne of the Majesty in the heavens."[30]

The Risen Lord is also important to the Church on earth. In fact, the church is said to be **his** church: "I will build my church . . ."[31] When Jesus promised that in the midst of as few as three persons, he would be present, the church has taken this very seriously. In a definite spiritual sense, Christians believe that Christ is among them as they read of him in Scripture, as they pray in his name and worship him. In witnessing, that is sharing the gospel in pro- clamation and deeds of love and reconciliation, Christ is also present, "to the end of the age." His supportive presence actually emboldens Christians to stand against severe challenges and negative circumstances. Some affirm his presence as the "Spirit of Christ", synonymous with the Holy Spirit, while others understand it as a particular way the unseen Lord himself is present.

For a majority of Christians, the Sacrament of Communion or the ordi- nance of the Lord's Supper is the definitive way in which Jesus is present among his people. When he passed the bread and the cup among his disciples and asked them to "do this in remembrance of me,"[32] he instituted a practice that would convey his presence long after the Passover Meal. The Apostle Paul reinforced this by telling the Corinthians that "as often as you do this, you show the Lord's death till he returns."[33] Many Christians follow the Aristotelian understanding of Thomas Aquinas who taught that there was a requisite mysterious transformation of the bread and wine into the actual body and blood of Christ which Aquinas called "transubstantiation." The Feast of Corpus Christi, which celebrates in the Eastern Orthodox Churches the public parade of the sacred elements of the Eucharist, is a rich annual experience of the encounter of believers with the sacramental elements of bread and wine. Still others prefer to understand the presence of Christ as an "anamnetic moment" wherein communicants in the Supper reenact the Supper in such a vivid way that the reenactment actually contains the life of Christ in itself. This was the position of the Swiss reformer Huldrych Zwingli and subsequently many Protestants.

But, there are other ways in which Jesus is known in the church and beyond in contemporary Christian thought. For instance, Christ as a symbol through his name, through preaching, and visual reminders like the cross, speak of God's healing in a world of violence; he provides a word of reconciliation and peace that advances God's new creation, and he stands with those who are oppressed. This last aspect of a mission among the oppressed is particularly relevant in Latin American Christology and the Black liberation experience. To say that "Christ is risen" is a powerful statement that shakes institutions to their foundations, asserts Church of England Bishop N. T. Wright.[34] In the context of Latin American poverty and political oppression, it is the living Christ who urges the church to stand for the cause of the poor. Similarly, Black theologians see the Living Christ as the voice within the church that seeks to uncover and reveal oppression and racism as seen in North American and South African cultures.

For many Christians, there continues to be a mystical presence of Christ in their individual lives. When the Apostle Paul wrote to the Church at Colossae, of the mystery of Christ: "Christ in you the hope of glory," he was pointing to an experiential reality. As Christ dwells corporately in his church and individually in each Christian, it is Christ who compels Christians to proclaim his message and Christ who calls Christian believers toward a fully mature religious experience. This causes Christians to speak of their personal relationship with Jesus, their walk with Jesus, and the voice of Jesus in their lives.

On the leading edge of Christian theology is the question of the finality of Christ in a world of religions. A strong, explicit doctrine of Christ leads to an exclusivistic understanding of Christianity. Many Christians believe that the message of God in Christ is the only religious answer to the human quest for salvation. However, an open Christology leads to convergences with other religions. For instance, Karl Rahner and the theologians of the Roman Catholic Vatican II school propose that Christ is the fullness of God's truth and grace and that there is truth in other religions that is somehow compatible with Christian beliefs about Christ. In another vein, John Hick builds upon a Platonic understanding of Christ, and believes that "Christ" is a statement that God is a center around whom all religions revolve. From this perspective, Jesus Christ points to a universal truth in God, not to an exclusive pathway to salvation through one religious tradition. Thus the meaning of Jesus spans a wide variety of possibilities in historic and contemporary Christian thinking.

Paul: The second generation

Arguably, Christianity would not be quite what it is without the singularly important work of Paul the Apostle. He was the chief interpreter of record, the principal theological interpreter of Jesus' teachings, an energetic missionary who carried the gospel throughout the Empire, and the apostolic glue that held together a very disparate community from Jerusalem to Spain. More than anything else, he is the leading character in the formal account of the expansion of Christianity as related in the Book of Acts. Christians revere Paul in a number of ways, from including several of his letters in the New Testament to quoting his words on the definitions of key ideas, and even in naming churches and persons after him. He is, by the way, the only personality of the New Testament era for whom there is a description of his physical characteristics.

Born in the city of Tarsus in Asia Minor, Saul was a Hellenistic Jew and Roman citizen who made his living by making tents. He had a sister who lived in Jerusalem and who was likely the reason for his moving away from his home at an early age to study. He probed the Jewish scriptures under a rabbi named Gamaliel and specialized in the Psalms. At length, he became a member of the Pharisee sect. In the early days of the Christian movement, Saul was a leading agent of persecution, complicit, for instance, in the stoning of Stephen, the first Christian martyr. Saul's entire orientation changed in a moment during a journey to Damascus where he claimed to have encountered the risen Lord Jesus. He was temporarily blinded and sought counsel from a Christian disciple in Damascus, Ananias. Ananias instructed Saul in the emerging tradition, baptized him, and introduced him to the Christian community in Damascus. At some point in his early Christian development, Saul changed his name to Paul, perhaps to identify his new Christian identity.

Paul began preaching about Jesus to the Jewish community in Damascus and encountered fierce opposition as one who had betrayed his earlier reputation. He next went to Jerusalem to join the core of Jesus' disciples and, even given his powerful personal testimony, he was rejected as an enemy. Barnabas, one of the leading disciples at Jerusalem, took Paul under his wing, but in general, those at Jerusalem remained doubtful. They recommended that Paul return to his home village in Tarsus, presuming that among his kin, he would recant his Christian conversion. Later he spent time in Arabia where he had further revelations about God and Jesus. After 14 years, Paul visited Jerusalem again to meet with Peter and James, the brother of Jesus, who was a leading elder in the church there.

About 46–48 CE, Paul took a lengthy journey through Syria, Cilicia (southeastern Turkey), and Galatia. He preached among the Gentiles and basically turned away from the Jewish community. He made a second trip to Jerusalem in 49 CE where he was part of a discussion with leading apostles about admitting Gentiles as equal members of the Christian community. He was involved in a later debate with Peter over dining with Gentiles. At Antioch, Paul finally received acceptance in the larger Christian community and began a far-ranging second missionary journey throughout Asia and Greece.

He visited Philippi, Thessalonika, Corinth, Ephesus, and Macedonia. During a third trek to Jerusalem, he was arrested on charges of sedition, profaning the temple, and being a ringleader of a sect called the Nazarenes, and he was imprisoned at Caesarea. He claimed Roman citizenship and appealed to Rome, the right of every citizen. Under armed guard he was escorted to Rome where he was under house arrest for 2 years, 60–62 CE. Paul was most likely executed at Rome during the Neronian Persecution in 62 CE.

Pauline Christianity

Most interpreters of Paul's thought see several important characteristics at work. First, Paul's thinking about God emerges from his correspondence with churches. From his first letter to the Thessalonians, to his letters to Rome and the Philippians, a period of perhaps a decade, Paul's thinking shows three critical points: his own conversion, his interaction with the senior apostles at Jerusalem, and the incident at Antioch where he was confronted with the seeming conflict between law and grace. Major changes in Paul's thinking involve the nearness of the return of Jesus, his understanding of suffering, and his belief that justification was by faith alone. As Pauline theologian James Dunn has argued, what was always stable for Paul was Christ: "Christ is the thread which runs through all, the lens through which all comes into focus, the glue which bonds the parts into a coherent whole."[35]

Paul was an exponent of the role of Jesus as God's Son through whom salvation was freely offered. He claimed, however, to have received further information as a revelation from God. This included his priority of law over grace, a call for a distinctive Christian lifestyle, his understanding of the practice of the Lord's Supper, a particular eschatology, and his insights into Jesus as the Christ. One of the outstanding features of Paul's thought was the new vocabulary he brought to the Christian movement: gospel, grace, faith, love, sin, the body, and church. In a very real sense, Paul laid out the categories of Christian theology.

Trained as a Pharisee, Paul appreciated the importance of the law in Jewish thought. Yet, he learned through his own experience the overarching relevance of grace. He wrote to the Galatian Christians that the law was a schoolteacher to bring persons to Christ, with faith being a more mature understanding.[36] To the Ephesian Christians he underscored the free gift of salvation in Christ, and he wrote to the Romans that a person is "justified by faith."[37] Ironically, he came into conflict with more consistent Jewish Christians like Peter and

James in Jerusalem who wanted to maintain certain dietary rules, the rite of circumcision, and a position that accredited faithful works in pleasing God. Paul held his position, however, and managed to influence a succession of "Paulinists" like Marcion, Augustine, Luther, Calvin, and the Reformed Tradition. One wonders what Christianity would have looked like if Saul had not been converted.

Paul's version of Christianity assumed that sufficient time would transpire for persons to "grow in the faith and knowledge of Jesus Christ." In the case of the Christians at Corinth, he noted immature, divisive behavior that he likened to "babes in Christ." Elsewhere he wrote of sanctification, a process of becoming set apart to God in holiness and lifestyle. Paul was critical of worldliness and chastised believers for engaging in worldly or sinful practices from eating meat sacrificed to idols, drunkenness, personal immorality, and unkind, ungenerous attitudes.

One of the categories of Paul's thought that provokes an ongoing debate, pertains to his views on last things. Paul was at first captive to a Hebraic idea about the coming of Messiah, but he moved to recognize the need for a "fullness of time." This created a tension between the present and an age to come—as one theologian puts it, an "already-not-yet" set of circumstances. This tension would generate even more distinctions, such as the differences between what Paul called the "flesh" and his discussion of the "spirit."[38] Eventually, Paul (and those who wrote in his train) created a highly specialized eschatology that involved a clash of evil and good, a special place and role for the Church at the return of Christ, and a judgment at the end of all things. His words to an anxiety-ridden group at Thessalonika led to new details about the last days before the judgment of God. We shall discuss this in detail in Chapter 6.

Finally, Paul's writings are crucial in the development of the church. More than Jesus' words, or any other apostle, Paul was definitive in what he wrote about the origin, purposes, and future of the church. He introduced several metaphors for the church's identity. Called variously the "Body of Christ," saints, the "field of God," the building of God, God's temple, and the "Bride of Christ," the church is the people of God, redeemed by Christ at both a local congregational level, and in a universal way. The origin of the church lay in God's predestinated plan to redeem a peculiar group of people for God. God knew who these people were, sent his Son, Jesus, to redeem them, and present them back to God "without spot, blemish or wrinkle," to use Paul's words to the church at Ephesus.[39] For Paul, the true church should be engaged in a holy "walk," worthy of their calling and recognizing the temptations presented by the world, bodily desires, and the devil. Rather than giving place to unrighteousness, according to Paul, Christians should be filled with the Spirit, avoid grieving the Spirit, and walk according to the guidance of the Spirit. Paul used colorful metaphors in discussing the expectations laid upon believers and the church, including the armour of a Roman soldier and the race that a competitive runner makes.

In his correspondence with the Christians at Corinth, Paul laid down an order for the celebration of the Lord's Supper that would in time become sacramental. The understanding that he claimed to have received directly from the Lord Jesus was more than a mere recollection or reenactment of a Passover Meal. Rather, it was the proclamation of a new covenant with God in Christ that was to be proclaimed as a witness until the return of Jesus. Significantly, in the context of church life, Paul attached the occurrence of sickness to impious actions among believers with the resulting need for repentance. He thus added to the contemporary practices the important element of self-examination. This would evolve in the historical development of the sacrament as a requirement of confession, penance, and absolution.

An unusual man in any assessment, Paul suffered a lack of esteem among some Christians that caused him to assert from time to time the authority of his own experiences. He wrote to the Galatians about his sojourn in Arabia to convince them of his having received a special revelation by being caught up into a "third heaven." In correspondence attributed to Paul, his understudy, Timothy, was urged to emulate Paul's model leadership and lifestyle (II Timothy 2.2). Somewhat petulantly, he recounted to the Corinthians his own record of accomplishments in the gospel:

> I am speaking as a fool—I dare to boast. Are they Hebrews? So am I. Are they Israelites? So am I. Are they descendents of Abraham? So am I. Are they ministers of Christ? I am talking like a madman—I am a better one: with far greater labors, far more imprisonments, with countless floggings, and often near death. Five times I have received from the Jews the forty lashes minus one. Three times I was beaten with rods. Once I received a stoning. Three times I was shipwrecked; for a night and a day I was adrift at sea; on frequent journeys, in danger from rivers, danger from bandits, danger from my own people, danger from Gentiles, danger in the city, danger in the wilderness, danger at sea, danger from false brothers and sisters; in toil and hardship, through many a sleepless night, hungry and thirsty, often without food, cold and naked. And besides, I am under daily pressure because of my anxiety for all the churches . . .[40]

Paul's legacy continues to be seen across Christianity. His ideas about predestination were picked up in the writings of St. Augustine in the fifth century and again emphasized in the sixteenth century by John Calvin and the Reformed tradition. Paul's ethical standards about everything from congregational leadership, the role of women, and human sexuality, remain standards for a strictly bible-based system of Christian decision-making. His understanding of salvation achieved through simple faith became the mantra for the Reformation. The Pauline statement on Christology became an insight into the fuller meaning of Jesus as Christ:

> Let this mind be in you, which was also in Christ Jesus,
> Who, being in the form of God,
> Thought it not robbery to be equal with God,
> But made himself of no reputation, and
> Took upon him the form of a servant, and
> Was made in the likeness of men; and
> Being found in fashion as a man
> Humbled himself and became obedient unto death,
> Even the death of a cross.[41]

'Historical Jesus' refers to attempts to "reconstruct the life & teachings of Jesus of Nazareth by critical historical methods"

In summary

This chapter began with the assertion that understanding the importance of Jesus of Nazareth is vitally important to understanding Christianity. Yet, one finds that among comparative Christian scholarship, there is much debate about Jesus. For instance, internationally renowned English New Testament theologian, George Beasley-Murray, stated, "The twentieth century has been marked from its outset . . . by an uncertainty as to who Jesus was. This uncertainty has been acute among New Testament scholars and has spread among theologians."[42] It is hardly the case that Christianity has swept away its perceived difficulties with unthinking theological confessions or coercive measures from a central religious authority. A contemporary philosophical theologian wonders why those who teach and write Christian doctrine pay so little attention to the large amount of good and widely read systematic accounts of the historical Jesus.[43]

The historical Jesus is a highly relevant issue for Christianity. Because there were virtually no written eyewitness accounts that survive to the life of Jesus, debate has first arisen over the texts and traditions that emerged in the first five decades. An initial task is to sort out the best manuscripts and establish the story line of Jesus' life. Next, one has to deal with the theological interpretation the early churches placed upon the life of Jesus. In addition to the life of Jesus, the life and work of Paul the Apostle comes into focus as a pillar of the Christian tradition. Scholars expend a good deal of effort in comparing the theological perspectives of Jesus and Paul in establishing the enduring tenets of Christianity. An enduring question remains over the degree to which Paul modified the teachings of Jesus or further elaborated Jesus' emphases.

Though there were numerous oral and literary traditions flowing into the kerygma or central teaching about Jesus, what emerged was a consensus that Jesus was a Son of Man and the Son of God. These titles/terms affirmed his humanness in the historical context of first century CE as a Jewish person of the lineage of the Tribe of Benjamin, as well as his being a divine person miraculously conceived through the Holy Spirit of God. Jesus' mission was to redeem Israel from their sinfulness and then uniquely to reconcile all persons to God.

For further reading and study

Bathrellos, Demetrius. *The Byzantine Christ: Person, Nature, and Will in the Christology of Saint Maximus the Confessor.* Oxford: Oxford University Press, 2004.

Beasley-Murray, George R. *Jesus and the Kingdom of God.* Grand Rapids, MI: Eerdmans, 1986.

Bruce, F. F. *The Pauline Circle.* Grand Rapids, MI: Eerdmans, 1985.

Bultmann, Rudolf K. *History of the Synoptic Tradition.* New York: Harper and Row, 1963.

Crossan, John Dominic. *Four Other Gospels: Shadows on the Contours of the Canon.* Minneapolis, MN: Winston Press, 1987.

Cupitt, Don. *Reforming Christianity.* Santa Rosa, CA: Polebridge Press, 2001.

Dunn, James D. G. *The Theology of Paul the Apostle.* Grand Rapids, MI: Eerdmans, 1998.

Dunn, James D. G. *The New Perspective on Paul.* Grand Rapids, MI: Eerdmans, 2008.

Ehrman, Bart D. *The New Testament: A Historical Introduction to the Early Christian Writings.* New York: Oxford University Press, 2004.

Funk, Robert W. *The Five Gospels: The Search for the Authentic Words of Jesus.* San Francisco, CA: Harper Collins, 1997.

Houlden, Leslie, editor. *Jesus in History, Thought, and Culture: An Encyclopedia.* 2 vols. Santa Barbara, CA: ABC-Clio, 2003.

Meeks, Wayne A. *The First Urban Christians: The Social World of the Apostle Paul.* New Haven, CT: Yale University Press, 2003.

Metzger, Bruce M. *The Text of the New Testament: Its Transmission, Corruption and Restoration.* New York: Oxford University Press, 2005.

Moltmann, Jürgen. *Jesus Christ for Today's World*. Minneapolis, MN: Fortress Press, 1994.

Reumann, John. *Jesus in the Church's Gospels: Modern Scholarship and the Earliest Sources*. Philadelphia, PA: Fortress Press, 1968.

Schillebeeckx, Edward. *Paul the Apostle*. New York: Crossroad, 1983.

Sloyan, Gerard. *Jesus: Word Made Flesh*. Collegeville, MN: Liturgical Press, 2008.

Stanton, Graham. *The Gospels and Jesus*. New York: Oxford University Press, 2002.

Tillich, Paul. *Systematic Theology,* Vol. II. Chicago, IL: University of Chicago Press, 1963.

Wright, N. T. *The Resurrection of the Son of God*. Minneapolis, MN: Augsburg Fortress Press, 2003.

Wuerthwein, Ernst. *The Text of the Old Testament: An Introduction to the Biblia Hebraica*. Grand Rapids, MI: Eerdmans, 1979.

2 Community and Structure

It is questionable that Jesus intended to start a permanent religious order, let alone a succession of priests or a political institution that would endure for at least 2,000 years. He seemed to be ruggedly anti-institutional in his critique of those who served the religious establishments of his day and his ridding the Temple in Jerusalem of marketing and money lending. Jesus was appreciative of the religious life of the Jewish synagogue, growing up in its midst and reading and preaching in it as a young man. Some Christian scholars have argued that the synagogue was the model on which the later structure of the church was based. There is in fact only one reference in the gospels that connects Jesus with the church during his human lifetime: "You are Peter, and upon this rock I will build my church, and the gates of Hades will not prevail against it."[1] Whether he was referring to the emerging institution or a simple assemblage of his followers, is a topic of useful debate.

The Church: A voluntary association

Christianity is at its essence a conglomeration of voluntary religious associations. It has a remarkable history of beginning as a Jewish rabbi's following, transformed into a network of religious associations throughout the expanse of the Roman Empire, later authorized by imperial edicts to become a religious institution, ultimately to be returned to its status as a network of complex voluntary associations. The heart of Christian organization and community is the *ecclesia*, literally "the called out ones," derived from a similar Hebrew term *qa'hal* that summoned an assembly of the people, for instance in the Sinai wilderness. In first century Greek usage, *ecclesia* was a gathering of citizens to conduct business that more often than not included religious activities.[2] A number of terms of cognate usage in Christian discourse have emerged from this seminal concept: ecclesiastical, ecclesial, ecclesiasticism, ecclesiology.

Jesus of Nazareth had a following that periodically expanded and contracted from a handful of 12 disciples to a throng of 500. On the road and close at hand were the select few that included fishermen, a tax collector, farmers, and tradesmen. An inner circle of Peter, James, and John were noted many times in the Gospel narratives. Doubtless, many others beyond the Twelve followed at a distance, from both Jewish and Gentile ethnic groups, particularly as he visited cities like those of the Decapolis and villages like Capernaum. Jesus' followers were disciplined by commandments, doctrines, stories, deep personal relationships, and remarkable experiences. Some understood his command to preach, teach, heal, and baptize as applying to their own missions in his name and authority. The duration of these early associations with Jesus of Nazareth was about 3 years, if one follows the reckoning of Jewish feasts in the gospel stories. After the death and resurrection of Jesus, many other converts to Jesus' "Way" came along, including the redoubtable Saul of Tarsus, one of the chief recorded exponents of the movement in the first century, as well as members of Jesus' own family like James his half brother. The associations began as outgrowths of Temple worshippers in Jerusalem and later synagogue worshippers from Palestine to Rome and beyond.

The ideal Christian community was, and is, a local assembly; in English, a church or congregation. Congregations met in homes and thus were 20–25 persons maximum. Relationships were likely by family or neighbors, and both women and men were leaders. As in the synagogue, an elder took responsibility for spiritual leadership, conducting worship and supervising care of members, relations with other assemblies and conflict resolution. The format was flexible in the first century, with prophets and teachers at Antioch and apostles and elders in Jerusalem. A second layer of congregational leadership soon emerged in the role of deacons (literally servants = *diaconos*) who cared for the Lord's Supper and the needs of widows and others in the congregations. In this twofold division of labor, the roots of a clergy type and the laity emerged, an important distinction in Church history.

Within a region, for instance Syria or Greek city-states like Corinth, clusters of congregations came under the influence of leading elders or apostles and literary traditions of the stories of Jesus or apostolic letters that came to assume authority. The tasks of monitoring correct belief, teaching new converts, discipline of wayward members, responding to heretical ideas, and supervision of local elders came to define a ministry of oversight or administration called bishops (*episcopos*). By the time of Polycarp of Smyrna (d.155), a bishop was the symbolic head of the churches in a region, likely elected by elders, then by other bishops. Predictably, in still larger regions of development, as Ephesus, Rome, or Antioch, yet another layer of supervision emerged as archbishops or metropolitans, the latter associated with cities. It is peculiarly evident by (250 CE) that the cities of Rome, Antioch, and Alexandria became "sees" or the major focal points of the Christian community. Authority passed from Jesus to the apostles, men who knew him or worked with him, these were followed by their protégés later called the "Apostolic Fathers," then bishops, archbishops, etc. It came to be an important issue to be able to identify a kind of dynastic succession of leaders to ratify the spiritual authority that later generations could trace directly to Jesus. This was called apostolic succession and was evident in the narrative that Eusebius crafted in his "first" history of the Christian Church (completed in 323 CE).

The rise of Christian political institutions

With the changes brought about during the reign of Constantine, Christianity entered a new era of complexity and influence. The voluntary associations gave way to a connection of parishes, dioceses, and archdioceses that looked ultimately to Rome for direction and definition. As early as 250 CE, Cyprian of Carthage in North Africa wrote of his belief in the unity of the

Church: "Whoever is separated from the Church and is joined to an adulteress, is separated from the promises of the Church . . . He can no longer have God for his father, who has not the Church for his mother."[3] Likewise, Irenaeus, Bishop at Lyon, and Tertullian also in North Africa and both in the second and third centuries, wrote in support of the unity of the Church and the ascendancy of Rome.

For Christian historians from Eusebius to the present, the Emperor Constantine has been seen as the fountainhead of political Christianity. It is clear in historical perspective that when Constantine came to realize the importance of the rising Christian community, a new era in institutionalization opened. His own "conversion" meant that imperial religion was broadened to include, rather than exclude, the Christian religion. From Constantine onwards, the emperors themselves would become characters on the stage of Christian history. Further, his interposition in the doctrinal controversies swirling around Arius that led to an ecumenical Christian council at Nicea insured the evolution of an imperial theology, especially given the enforcement procedures of Nicea lying with imperial edicts. Further, Constantine's reorganization of the church into a diocesan structure that imitated the old Roman imperial regions plus revenue advantages and other privileges for clergy were signs of the outset of the Constantinian era of Christianity. Church and state were thus wed as the Roman Empire moved into its twilight period politically.

The Christian Church by the demise of the Empire in 476 was the sole unifying force in Europe north of the Mediterranean from the British Isles to the Ural Mountains. In the wake of the decline of the Roman Empire, various tribes settled in patterns across Europe and created smaller jurisdictions. What unified the entire continent was the strength and spread of the Christian episcopacy, divided only by the Latin and Byzantine rites and episcopacies. Pope Gregory I (called the "Great") recognized the potential of a unified and vital organized Christianity and during his life embodied a linguistically, administratively, and pastorally united Christian world that mirrored the boundaries of the former Roman Empire. Moreover, the missionary expansion of Latin Christianity into the British Isles at the end of the sixth century, the virtual conversion of the Frankish Kingdom in the next hundred years, and the forays of missionaries from Rome and the Byzantine Empire as far to the Northeast as Poland in the ninth century and Kievan Rus in the tenth century sealed the political and cultural influence of Christianity upon the continent.

The coronation of Charlemagne remains the capstone of the early medieval kingdom of Christ. Charlemagne had his own grandiose territorial and military ambitions, but when he traveled to Rome in 799, rescuing Pope Leo III en route from thugs and his own unworthiness, Charlemagne managed to be acclaimed on Christmas Day, 800, "Charles Augustus, crowned by God as the great and pacific emperor,"[4] by the pope himself. Charlemagne's inheritance included restructuring of the church, strengthening its administrative powers and recognizing the importance of the monastic life, and setting high ideals for local clergy. Little wonder that he grew in importance from being the Christian ruler of settled tribes to the Christian emperor of a new Rome, a link not lost on history as successor to Constantine.

In the next 200 years, the institutional church reached a peak of power and authority, sanctioned by Christian political rulers. This period also witnessed times and events of extreme conflict and corruption. One important evidence of the institutional church's influence was in the development of monasteries—virtual kingdoms within the kingdom. Geographically dispersed throughout Europe and the British Isles, the Benedictine Rule had become the standard in the West and the Rule of St. Basil in the East. The monasteries were fully integrated into a fractured medieval social fabric, offering education for the wellborn, farming lands for families in a feudal system, and centers of spiritual disciplines, the sacraments, literature, and the arts. Along with the monasteries, the Episcopal system linked local and regional interests like no other institution. Bishops became feudal lords with priests as their vassals. Bishops received the support of kings and princes in return for legitimizing them. Bishops were more often in league with temporal princes than with Rome, and this meant a powerful partnership economically and militarily.

In the ninth and tenth centuries, the papacy made important strides in protection of its interests. Drawing upon spurious documents like the Donation of Constantine and the Pseudo-Isidorian Decretals, popes exercised their power in the coronation of kings, the arbitration of disputes, accountability of all bishops to Rome, and responsibility for the extension of the faith and Christian culture to the farthest boundaries of Europe, in this era, Poland, Scandinavia, and Britain.[5] To solidify the power of the papacy, key families in Italy and France came to control the choice of popes, notably the clan of Theophylact, later the Medici, and Otto the Great's family in the German kingdoms. More than this, in Rome an ecclesiocracy was quietly developing that included significant landholdings called the Papal Estates, a formidable home in the Lateran Palace, a library of the best manuscripts and ancient records, an art collection, and elaborate chapels and cemeteries. To administer papal affairs, a "curia" was set up of bureaus, courts, and collection agencies that were the marvel of European governments. At the top of the kingdom in the West sat the bishop of Rome, successor to the Apostle Peter.

Reforming trends and counter-movements

Any religious institution, by virtue of its human elements, is subject to error, overextension of prerogative, and corruption, and the Christian Church in the Middle Ages was no exception. Despite the changes that Charlemagne set in place, his successors Louis the Pious, Charles the Bald, and Lothair, managed to divide Charlemagne's Christian kingdom into smaller principalities, leaving Europe in a fractured and fragile condition, especially in view of the incursions of Danish-Norwegian Sea Peoples. One of the results was the reduction of social and economic life to a feudal system that emphasized local allegiances. Across the Latin Christian world, there was too little accountability of priests to the ideals of servant-hood, monastic life was burdened with immorality and broken rules, and the papacy became a pawn among Italian families and French and German kings and princes. Fortunately, in the Christian community there are opportunities for reform and stalwart figures who are willing to be heroic in calling the Church to return to the ideals of Jesus.

In the eleventh century, the results of widespread monastic reform through the Cluniac Movement were becoming evident. Founded by a pious lay patron, Duke William of Aquitaine, the Abbey at Cluny in Burgundy stood for celibacy, communal property, and full dedication of monks to intercessory prayer and worship. Its influence was churchwide. Among the parish priest-hood, the practice of payment for an ecclesiastical service, called simony, and the keeping of wives or concubines by the clergy, was brought into check. At the top of the Christian institutional hierarchy, the papacy underwent significant reform achieving a measure of independency for the holy office and bringing accountability down through the structures by instituting "cardinals" who would review and revise the offices of the papacy and even come to control the election of popes. Pope Leo IX took it upon himself to rid the priesthood of corrupt practices, to depose errant and defiant bishops, and to establish himself as the chief administrator of the church rather than being a mere apostolic symbol. Later, a Tuscan monk named Hildebrand who was to reign as Pope Gregory VI from 1073 to 1085, brought even greater attention to institutional reform. Hildebrand yearned for an ideal Christian society led by the Roman Church and a papacy with universal powers, including ultimate temporal authority over emperors. In a clash with German bishops and princes, Hildebrand tried to maintain papal supremacy by deposing Holy Roman Emperor Henry IV in 1076. A nasty collision of cultures, those of the German states and those siding with Rome and her allies, ensued. Having denounced the pope as a false monk, Henry prostrated himself before Gregory and asked for mercy. Four years later, the political slugfest repeated itself with the pope again deposing Henry, to which Henry responded by having a synod of bishops depose Gregory as pope, with a concocted successor-pope crowning Henry as Emperor in 1084. Ultimately, the issue of lay investiture of bishops continued through the twelfth century, but the power of the papacy in the lead of European politics and diplomacy was set by the reforming popes, as well as in the internal affairs of the Church.

The proclamation of the crusades marked an important chapter in the ability of Christianity to enforce its tenets. In the whirling events of medieval states, the Papacy reigned supreme in both earthly and spiritual matters and the popes had at their disposal the armies and princes of several kingdoms, notably in the Frankish and Italian principalities. By the tenth century, important territorial reconquests had been achieved in Sicily and the Iberian kingdoms. Likewise, in the East, church and state were united under the Emperors, although the Turkish armies posed a constant threat to their security. In the mid-eleventh century the two great Christian institutions, Latin Christendom and the Eastern Empire united to reconquer the Holy Lands in Palestine. Following an appeal from Alexis I in Constantinople to Pope Urban II in 1095, Urban proclaimed a crusade in which participants were promised complete remission of their sins under the right conditions of dying in battle. The response was dramatic and widespread and lasted in waves of enthusiasm for almost two centuries. Feudal nobility amassed armies and marched in heroic array, as did commoners, clerics, and even children. At length, the military pursuits produced marginal and reversed results, innocent children were taken into slavery, and a Latin Christian kingdom was set up in Jerusalem to administer politically what territorial gains were made. By all standards except one, the Crusades were a failure: no permanent territorial gains were made, Islam's advance was not arrested, the rift between the Eastern and Latin branches of Christendom was not healed, and personal gain out-distanced spiritual objectives. However, the Crusades did demonstrate the sheer authority and power of the institutional church to pull together people, resources, and kingdoms.

The period 1300 through 1500 saw two important trends in the rise of institutional Christianity, now referred to as "Christendom." First was an attempt to unite the Eastern and Western Churches that had suffered schism in 1054. Under pressure from encircling Turkish powers and an aggressive evangelization effort from Rome in the Baltic States and western Russia, the heads of the Eastern Churches met with papal representatives of Pope Eugenius IV at Florence in 1438–1439 to secure the support of the West in holding their territory. While the union achieved at the Council of Florence was denounced within decades and the popes were unable to send sufficient military presence to withstand the fall of Constantinople, the papacy itself was transformed into a universal headship of all Christendom. Thereafter, popes were to claim titles including Sovereign Pontiff, Vice-Regent and Vicar of Christ, Shepherd of all Christians, Ruler of the Church of God, excepting the rights and privileges of the patriarchs of the East. To many observers, this overreach of power from Rome amounted to an attempt to continue the imperial dream of pre-Christian Rome.[6]

The second trend reflected troubles at the very heart of the papal institution. From 1309 to 1377 the popes resided in the French city of Avignon, although holding the title of "bishops of Rome." This was ostensibly for security reasons, but actually reflected the control of the popes by French kings; it has been referred to as the "Babylonian Captivity" of the papacy. At the episcopal (bishops) and priestly levels, holding two or more appoint-ments, absenteeism, and loose moral conduct were widespread. Church offices were bought and sold, bribery in the election of popes took place, and prominent Italian families (the Borgias and Medici) controlled the candidates for cardinals and popes. Attempts to reform the papacy in a set of church-wide councils failed with the popes themselves becoming masters of the general councils. Perhaps most distressing was the decay of monastic houses, the luxury and laxity of the monastic lifestyle supposedly devoted to Christ, and the placement of younger daughters of the aristocracy in nunner-ies. By the late 1400s simony (fees for holding church offices) and the sale of indulgences (permits toward salvation) were common across the Western Church. Widespread discontent with Christendom prevailed as new national states emerged across the map of Europe.

The Reformations

Historians now speak of what was once referred to as the Protestant Reformation as a series of Reformations (Protestant and Catholic), each defined in broad sociopolitical terms and particularized in nation-states like England, Scotland, and Geneva and Zurich in Switzerland. In the space of less than a century, the unity of Latin Christianity was subjected to severe testing and broke into several pieces. New institutional development occurred among several groups who were defined by "confessions" or statements of doctrinal beliefs. In the East, the Orthodox churches remained unified and autonomous within states or "metropolitanates" and a convoluted decision-making process that assured that change was met within the context of the authority of the ancient Fathers.

Most accounts of the sixteenth century Age of Reform pay attention to earlier reforming trends seen in the lives of John Wycliffe and Jan Hus of Bohemia. Wycliffe, an Oxford lecturer and popular preacher in the 1370s, concluded that Scripture was a higher authority than the Church and particularly the papacy. Conceding the might of the popes as earthly leaders, Wycliffe called for the abolition of the papacy and the release of all church endowments. Ultimately, he wrote against transubstantiation and mendicant orders or friars, drawing to himself papal denunciations and charges of heresy. Although Wycliffe died of natural causes in 1484, the full punitive arm of the Roman Church came down on his reputation when the Bishop of Lincoln obeyed the edict of the Council of Constance and had Wycliffe's remains exhumed and burned in 1415. Hus, a Bohemian priest, was much influenced by Wycliffe's ideas through Wycliffe's wandering followers, the Lollards, and he drew the wrath of Rome as well. Hus held that Christ was the true head of the Church, the New Testament should be the foundation of Christian beliefs, and there was no validity to indulgences or the Church's use of coercion to enforce its edicts. Hus was judged to be a heretic in the train of Wycliffe and, condemned at the Council of Constance, he was burned at the stake in 1415. The reforms that Wycliffe and Hus thus advocated would wait another half century to have a solid impact upon the institutional Church.

Martin Luther remains the leading heroic figure of the Reformation. His unhappy spiritual pilgrimage that resulted in an evangelical breakthrough in the years 1513–1519, led him to question several abuses of his church. His program and writings to criticize and bring about reform led, however, to schism and a divided Christian world that separated "Protestants" from the

Roman and Catholic Church. The term "Protestant" applied to those followers of Luther and Zwingli at the Diet of Speyer in 1529 who protested actions in Roman Catholicism that were perceived to be contrary to the written Word of God. Luther held tenaciously to principles of the final authority of Holy Scripture, limitations upon papal prerogatives, a curbing of abuses like the sale of indulgences, and the theological principle that an individual person is justified by his faith, not by one's meritorious works or the sacraments. Luther's pilgrimage led him to find a new sense of Christian community on "reformed" principles like: the true church exists where the Word of God is rightly preached and the sacraments are correctly administered. His results were seen in the liberation of the Christian Church in many German states from Rome and a broadening movement that led to Scandinavia and the Americas known as Lutheranism.

The Age of Reform produced other significant figures as well. In the Swiss Confederacy, Huldrych Zwingli captained a reformed movement that drove back the armies of the papacy. Jean Calvin in France, and later Geneva, led in creating a Christian commonwealth that influenced Christianity in the Dutch provinces, Scotland, England, and North America. Most radical of all were disparate groups of "Anabaptists" (rebaptizers) who formed communities based on their reading of scripture and a pacifist yet socially transforming theology. Their communities were seen in the Dutch provinces, Switzerland, Bohemia, Poland, Italy, Russia, and the British Isles—literally wherever they could find safe havens. Reform came awkwardly to English Christianity when Henry VIII, formerly a defender of the Catholic faith, demanded accommodation for his marital cries from the Church and severed ties when Rome declined his requests. The reformed Church of England was perhaps the most variegated of all the Reformation churches, being influenced by both Lutheranism and Calvinistic thought. Finally, there was noticeable reform within the Roman Church in the pronouncement of the Council of Trent in 1565, the creation of the Society of Jesus, and the quiet work of thinkers like Therese of Avila and John of the Cross.

Significant to the dimension of Christian community, our topic in this chapter, was the institutional development that proceeded from the several streams of reformation. Lutherans reconstructed the parish system to provide for greater oversight of pastors and accountability to synods. They created a doctrinal standard to order their beliefs and enforce their reforms: the Augsburg Confession (1530). They also urged the establishment of universities and a spate of Lutheran and Reformed universities sprang up across central Europe. Calvin built a model religious culture in Geneva, shaped by a Christian Council, a university, and his own teaching ministry. His emphases led to universities and church structures in Holland, Scotland, and colonial America, with strong influences in Elizabethan England. The Calvinistic confessions, Belgic, Helvetic, and Westminster, insured doctrinal solidarity. The Radical reformers achieved a deeper sense of the individual congregation as community and of the individual himself, albeit in a fragmented and isolated set of experiences and confessional statements.

The upset created in the surges of reform affected Christendom in different ways. Among Roman Catholics resurgence occurred with institutions like the Jesuit missions, the Inquisition, and through the Jesuits, several new universities and theological seminaries. The Council of Trent reinforced and strengthened Catholic dogma and tradition and set it aright after absorbing the critiques of the reformers. Unlike the Western Catholic Church, however, the Eastern Churches did not undergo any comparable ecclesiological or doctrinal crises, and thus avoided the opportunity for self-criticism.[7] The Eastern Churches remained the "ancient Church," the true spiritual community in a divine cosmos all by itself.

For some within the reformation traditions, this would be positively labeled confessional or denominational Christianity, assuming a comprehensive view of the Christian religion that was manifested in various confessions or "denominated" bodies. For others, it was a bitter example of the sinful tendencies toward schism brought about by technological and commercial advances, economic greed, nationalism, clash of cultures, and overarching abuses of church power. In the West, the Roman Catholic Church maintained its self-image as the only true church and in fact continued to include the numerical majority of Christians worldwide.

The impact of religious diversity

The Reforming movements of the sixteenth century ratified the diversification of the Christian tradition. With European expansion into North America and later Asia, Australia, and Africa, the Christian community developed a polyglot identity. This was especially the result of the frontier experience in North America and the achievement of religious toleration in England in the latter decades of the seventeenth century.

The English, and to a lesser extent Swedish and Dutch, colonies in America provided the context for confessional variety and great toleration.

Congregationalists, Presbyterians, Quakers, Baptists, and Anglicans came to live more or less peaceably in New England. In the American Middle Colonies, Quakers, Reformed groups, Lutherans, and Catholics settled next to each other. In this region, the diversity also included smaller sects like Moravians, Brethren, Swedenborgians, German Pietists, and various millennialists and perfectionists. In the Southern colonies, for a time the Church of England was predominant, to be forced by the mid-eighteenth century to be tolerant of Baptists, Methodists, enthusiasts, and others. At the same time of colonial settlement, dissenting forces in England were eroding the idea of establishment to the point where in 1689 the Act of Toleration made it possible for most mainstream confessing Christians to live peaceably. This, coupled with the codification of religious freedom in the new United States of America constitution of 1789, assured that a variegated and voluntaristic form of Christianity would dominate the futures of Christian Europe and the Americas. Beyond the Appalachian Mountains in the interior, the greatest variety of all occurred. There Methodists, Mormons, Churches of Christ and odd varieties of Baptists and Perfectionists thrived. Each in course built institutions of missionary, educational, and administrative kinds.

Another example of the English-speaking varieties of Christianity was seen in Australia. Following the earliest settlements after 1788, the typical categories of Church of England and Dissent planted congregations in New South Wales, Tasmania, Victoria, and Western Australia. The primary Dissenting groups were Methodists, Presbyterians, and Baptists. Roman Catholicism in early Australia was associated with Irish immigrants. The British character of Christianity was also dominant in New Zealand, settled on the Australian pattern from the 1830s. Colonization in these two regions was more of a determining factor in how Christianity developed than sheer evangelization of aboriginal peoples.

Christianity reached Asia early and later in the missionary movements and progressed to an institutional stage in several nations and kingdoms. The first Catholic Christian missionaries to China were likely the Nestorians in the seventh century. Later, Catholic Christians reached China via the Silk Road across Asia in the thirteenth century via the Franciscan Order. Serious attempts at Christianization occurred beginning in 1552 with the Jesuits and in 1807 with the London Missionary Society. Baptists from England and later the United States supported missionaries to India from 1792, then Siam, Burma, China, Japan, Korea, and the Philippines. They were joined by most Protestant groups from England, Scotland, Germany, the Netherlands, and the

United States. Observably, competitive Christian subcultures were erected through publication of literature, associations of congregations, and educational institutions, though Christianity remains a minority religious tradition in Japan.

In South America, given the dominance of Roman Catholic missions from the sixteenth through the late nineteenth centuries, Christianity was monolithic until the Protestant evangelization of Argentina, Chile, Brazil, and Bolivia. A special instance of the Christian variety experience in Latin America occurred in Bolivia. As mining ventures required more technical workers and engineers, Scottish, English, Welsh, and American emigrants moved into regions like Sucre, Santa Cruz, and Oruro. With them came denominations like Presbyterians, Brethren, and Baptists. Baptists from Canada were quite influential in establishing a Liberal political tradition in Bolivia that called for religious toleration in a previously monolithic Catholic culture. In addition to the long-established episcopal and diocesan structures plus educational institutions of the Roman tradition, Protestants opened scores of academies, colleges, and theological schools in every Latin American nation.

By the twentieth century, the Christian community was recognizable in the great institutional denominations that competed with each other in wealth, population, and extent, as well as sects, congregations, mystics, and individualized communities. The structures followed the time-honored experience of congregations, regional organizations, and national bodies. Three types had won recognition for effectively defining the community: the episcopal (Roman Catholic, Church of England, Lutheran), the presbyterial/connectional (Presbyterian, Reformed, Methodist), and the Congregational (Congregationalists, Baptists, evangelicals). Owing to the influence of democratic social and political forces in the contexts, plus the general adaptability of the polity, the greatest amount of energy by 1900 was seen in the congregational forms of organization. H. Richard Niebuhr has offered an alternative to this traditional structural understanding of European and North American denominations by classifying the various groups according to socioeconomic profiles. Thus, Quakers, Baptists, early Methodists, and the Salvation Army are "churches of the disinherited" or lower classes; later Methodists in the United States and various kinds of Calvinists constitute a middle class; and Lutherans, Catholics, Scottish Presbyterians, and Orthodox make up the historic "immigrant" churches.[8] Whether one uses a theological model, or takes account of structural differences or socioeconomic factors, the reality is that American Christians (and likely others where research would ratify the conclusions) are highly differentiated in worship style, theological emphases, social ethics, and educational criteria for leadership. It would almost appear that in a given village or urban context where a variety of denominations exist, certain Christian groups (e.g., Roman Catholics and Quakers or Lutherans and Salvation Army) are so different that they represent different religious traditions altogether. One has to look carefully at an affirmation of Jesus Christ as a centering point in order to find a common denominator.

The ecumenical community

The notion of a globally interconnected Christian community is not new. One finds in the New Testament a desire among regional elders to meet at Jerusalem. Later, gatherings were held beginning an **ecumenical** (literally "world household") tradition. The Roman Catholic Church assumed the nature of community thus achieved and the Reformations broke that unity to a certain extent by independent confessional ideas of the church. At the commencement of the twentieth century, however, largely growing out of the Protestant missionary contexts in Asia, India, and Africa, a new sense of desire for a world community emerged. Steps were taken in 1905 with the International Missionary Council, convened at Amsterdam by J. H. Oldham and John R. Mott. Next was a regular meeting among church leaders labeled as the Faith and Order Movement in 1927 and 1937 by the Life and Work Movement. These three strands culminated in the first assembly of the World Council of Churches at Amsterdam in 1948. Representatives of all the church or ecclesial bodies gathered for celebration and consultation. Subsequent assemblies of the world Christian community convened at Stockholm, Canberra, Vancouver, Nairobi, and New Delhi. Even among the staunchest opponents of the formal ecumenical tradition, there were evidences of a desire for a global Christian community, notably in the World Association of Evangelicals and the Lausanne Conference meetings, the latter convened by American evangelist Billy Graham.

The Christian communities in India, China, and Australia, with their particular histories, became catalysts toward an ecumenical religious community. The missionary churches of India, often competing against each other and within themselves, began to coalesce in the creation of the Church of South India in 1947 followed by the Church of North India in 1970. This involved most of the European Protestant denominations, Presbyterians, Lutherans, Methodists, Baptists, and Congregationalists. In China during the period 1949–1954, Christian missions came to a halt at the insistence of a Marxist government under Mao Tse Tung. Later in the 1960s, a sharp crackdown came against Christians in the Cultural Revolution that led to imprisonment, disruption of church life, and closure of institutions. With economic and regime modernization in the 1990s, Christianity joined other Chinese religious cultures in a postdenominational age that banned all external interferences. Cooperation in the Three Self Church and the Amity Foundation led to Chinese Christianity once again emerging as a recognized community in that country. In Australia, Roman Catholic presence grew through post–World War II immigration, while overall Protestantism declined. An indigenization process occurred whereby the Church of England became the Anglican Church of Australia in 1981 and three denominations—Methodist, Presbyterian, and Congregationalist—came together as the Uniting Church of Australia in 1977.

One of the driving forces toward a greater recognition of the world Christian community is the realization that there is around Christianity a plurality of religious traditions. The World's Parliament of Religions held at Chicago, Illinois, in 1893 demonstrated this and even more so its successor the 2003 Parliament of World's Religions. Another factor certainly is the series of crises to which most of the Christian community feel obligated to respond. The issues include world peace and order, environmental hazards, and famine and hunger. Driven by the agenda of the United Nations, global Christians have become much more unified in their assertion of human rights. Finally, the development of the internet, rapid travel, and instantaneous communication has all facilitated an international Christian community in ways never before dreamt of.

In summary

Christians have a strong sense of community. From their earliest voluntary associations that amounted to house assemblies, they believe that gathering for worship and learning is vital to their experience. Holding that the Risen Lord is in their midst in one form or another, they are empowered spiritually beyond mere friendship or liturgical bonds. The Christian movement was largely a conglomeration of associations until recognized by the Emperor Constantine as a major religious force in the Roman Empire.

Constantinian Christianity, so-called, brought with it a long buildup toward institutionalization. The dispersed structure of the episcopacy enabled a connectedness that gave solidarity to leadership, belief, and practice of ritual. The development of monastic communities throughout the Christian world was a second permanent institution that made concrete the Christian ideal of community. The apogee of Christian community came in the papacy of the Roman Catholic Church in the West, where the bishops of Rome became the superior pastors and administrators of the entire Church. Adding to the spiritual authority of the popes was their accumulated temporal authority, granted to them through hard-fought battles with political rulers. In the East this was mirrored in the patriarchates and their close relationship with Byzantine and Russian emperors.

The Age of Reform in the sixteenth century fractured the unity of Christianity as existing in two communities (East and West), and led to even greater institutionalization. As a result of the Council of Trent, even the Roman Catholic Church followed the pattern of confessionalism and reform. Each of the confessional bodies that emerged from the Reformations achieved rather quickly an episcopacy, educational structures, and missionary organizations. Each possessed a kind of unity within its confession. Under the influence of the Enlightenment, Christianity at large became "modern," that is structurally and nationally defined and competitive within itself. Germany had its Evangelical Lutheran Church in many German states, while separate Lutheran churches existed for Sweden, Norway, Denmark, Iceland, Estonia, and Finland. There were separate Reformed churches in several German states, Switzerland, Scotland, Holland, and England.

The political achievement of religious freedom served only to strengthen the competitive spirit. In England, Ireland, and Wales religious toleration brought a resurgence of growth to the nonconformist sects of the late seventeenth and early eighteenth centuries. Baptists, Presbyterians, and Congregationalists were the primary beneficiaries of the numerical growth, but not left behind were Quakers and even Roman Catholics where they constituted a minority group. In the American colonies where an open frontier beckoned new growth and religious disestablishment became the law of the land in the 1790s, each group set out an agenda to become a leading force in the advance of Christianity in North America. Congregationalists and Presbyterians competed for the same geographical territory, as did Lutherans and German Reformed, while Methodists, Disciples of Christ, and Baptists competed for the same individual souls.

In the twentieth century, the Christian structures have seen something of a return to a sense of global community. The Protestant yearning for unity, realized in the World Council of Churches in 1948, drew to itself both the Orthodox and Roman Catholic Churches. Smaller bodies of evangelical Christians have likewise sought out each other to create community across structures and national boundaries. By its nature, Christianity is communal.

For further reading and study

Ascough, Richard S. *What Are They Saying About the Formation of the Pauline Churches?* New York: Paulist Press, 1998.

Brackney, William H. *Christian Voluntarism: Theology and Praxis*. Grand Rapids, MI: Eerdmans, 1996.

Cyprian. *Treatise I*: "On the Unity of the Church," in Alexander Roberts and James Donaldson, editors. *Ante-Nicene Fathers*, volume 5. Peabody, MA: Hendrickson Publishers, 423, 1999.

Davis, Leo D. *The First Seven Ecumenical Councils (325–787): Their History and Theology*. Wilmington, DE: Michael Glazier, 1987.

Frend, W. H. C. *The Early Church*. Philadelphia, PA: Fortress Press, 1984.

Gerrish, Brian A. *The Old Protestantism and the New: Essays in the Reformation Heritage*. Edinburgh: T&T Clark, 1982.

Hall, Douglas John. *The End of Christendom and the Future of Christianity*. Valley Forge, PA: Trinity Press International, 1997.

Harland, Philip A. *Associations, Synagogues, and Congregations: Claiming a Place in Ancient Mediterranean Society*. Minneapolis, MN: Fortress Press, 2003.

Hillerbrand, Hans J. *The World of the Reformation*. New York: Charles Scribner's Sons, 1973.

Hurtado, Larry. *At the Origins of Christian Worship: The Content and Character of Earliest Christian Devotion*. Grand Rapids, MI: Eerdmans, 1999.

Latourette, Kenneth S. *History of the Expansion of Christianity*. New York: Harper Brothers, 1943–1945.

Latourette, Kenneth S. *A History of Christianity*. New York: Harper and Row, 1953.

Lindberg, Carter. *The European Reformations*. Oxford: Blackwell, 1996.

Lynch, Joseph H. *The Medieval Church: A History*. London: Longman Group, Ltd., 1992.

Morris, Colin. *The Papal Monarchy: The Western Church from 1050 to 1250*. Oxford: The Clarendon Press, 1989.

Neill, Stephen, and Rouse Ruth. *A History of the Ecumenical Movement*. 3 vols. Geneva: World Council of Churches, 2004.

Niebuhr, Richard H. *The Social Sources of Denominationalism*. New York: Henry Holt and Company, 1929.

Ozment, Stephen. *The Age of Reform*. New Haven, CT: Yale University Press, 1980.

Schmemann, Alexander. "The Missionary Imperative in the Orthodox Tradition," in Daniel B. Clendenin, editor. *Eastern Orthodox Theology: A Contemporary Reader*. Grand Rapids, MI: Baker Books, 196, 1995.

Vallee, Gerard. *The Shaping of Christianity: The History and Literature of Its Formative Centuries 100–800.* New York: Paulist Press, 1999.

Walker, Williston, Norris, Richard A., Lotz, David W., and Handy, Robert T. *A History of the Christian Church.* Fourth Edition. New York: Charles Scribner's Sons, 1985.

Williams, George H. *The Radical Reformation.* Kirksville, MO: Truman State University Press, 2000.

3 Religious Values, Theology, and Ethics

As the noted comparative religionist Wilfred Cantwell Smith has pointed out, the consequences of a religious tradition are at least as important as its background.[1] Christian thinkers and the community at large have produced a fairly coherent set of values that meet the important concerns and questions of a religious tradition. These values have transformed hundreds of generations of Christians. From Paul of Tarsus to the contemporary scene, a peculiar theology or set of teachings has grown up to become the substance of Christian ideology. Uniquely, Christians have an orientation to the world, a lifestyle, and set of standards and expectations about how Christians ought to live and what the world should look like if significantly influenced by their values. This last aspect has become a field of inquiry and comment in itself, namely Christian ethics. Overall, it is important to note that modern Christianity is a self-critical religious tradition, by which it is meant that Christian thinkers, within the community and critics without, are able to critique and evaluate Christianity without fear of reprisal.

The great religious questions and concerns

According to Paul Tillich, religion attempts to respond to the concerns of humanity that are of ultimate concern.[2] These may be phrased in the form of questions: "What is the origin of life?" "What is the fulfillment or destiny of humanity?" "If there is meaning beyond me, how do I understand it and what is my response to that reality?", and "what is my value and purpose?" Religion as a sense of ultimate dependence, as Frederich Schleiermacher wrote, helps to direct the religious quest to something or someone higher or more powerful than oneself.

Christians respond to the first query by sharing with Judaism a monotheistic worldview. Christians agree with Jewish cosmology that the world and life within it has its origin in something larger that has brought it into being, whom they believe is personal and referred to as "God," the "Lord," or Yahweh. The idea of creation is affirmed: a series of God's acts that shaped the physical universe, and started life at least on planet earth. The opening chapters of Genesis are definitive, and yet pregnant with mystery:

> In the beginning God created the heaven and the earth. And the earth was without form and void; and darkness was upon the face of the deep. And the Spirit of God moved upon the face of the waters . . . These are the generations of the heavens and of the earth when they were created, in the day that the Lord God made the earth and the heavens. And the Lord God formed man of the dust of the ground and breathed into his nostrils the breath of life and man became a living soul. (Genesis 1:1–2; 2: 4, 7)

Similarly, Christians hold a view that human destiny is gradually pursuing fulfillment in the purposes of the same God who brought it into being. St. Augustine, bishop and theologian in North Africa, put it this way, "You hast made us for yourself and our hearts are restless until they find rest in You." Later, Thomas Aquinas, an equally important voice from the medieval Christian tradition, wrote, "The ultimate end of man we call beatitude. For a man's happiness or beatitude consists in the vision whereby he sees God in his essence."[3] To which C. S. Lewis, a twentieth-century Anglican lay theologian added, "If we discover a desire within that nothing can satisfy, also we should begin to wonder if perhaps we were created for another world."[4]

For practicing Christians, it is insufficient merely to hold a view or perspective and not respond to it in action or behavior. Consequently, Christians are on a lifelong and historic quest to find God in relationships with God and among each other. Moreover, Christians think of their presence in the world as a kind of manifestation of God's presence or kingdom in reality.

Satisfaction in the Christian community as to the great religious questions of humanity amounts to a sense of being at peace with God, meaning that a person is not alienated from God, and is essentially free of anxiety about one's destiny and value. This is achieved by a devotional life through prayer, the sacraments, and reading and responding to Scripture, performing deeds of virtue, and having one's basic religious convictions reinforced in a group context. As several theologians have concluded, all Christian doctrine is mediated in experience.

Christian theology

Theology in Christian usage refers to the organized teachings or doctrines of the tradition. Christian theology is derived from the content of the Old and New Testaments, the interpretations of centuries of teachers, and ratified in the practices of the Christian community. Among Orthodox Christians, theology is heavily weighted toward the first six centuries and summarized in the creeds. For Roman Catholics, theology is a combination of the teachings of Scripture as interpreted by the Fathers (early writers of the churches), summarized in the creeds and council pronouncements, by canon law, and revised from time to time by papal and conciliar decrees, such as Vatican II. Among Protestants, there is a strong dependence upon Scripture alone, though the creeds are guides and there is a mainstream consensual interpretation of Scripture that has emerged from the magisterial reformers of the sixteenth century and their major followings since (Martin Luther, John Calvin, Huldrych Zwingli). From the fourth century, the principle of orthodoxy is central to correct doctrine; for the Reformers it is absolute conformity to the Scriptures.

At the heart of Christian doctrine is the declaration of one God: God has many names in the Hebrew Scriptures that Christians believe reveal God's activities toward humankind: Elyon (Most High God); Shaddai (Almighty

God); Olam (Everlasting God), for instance. But, God is also essentially a mystery and Christians appreciate the respect that Jewish theologians pay to God by revering God's name: YHWH.[5] Christians prefer to talk about God as "Lord" (Adonai), and they pray to God as Jesus instructed them in the name of "Father" (literally in English "daddy"). God is Creator and Lord God, sovereign of the universe. Unique to a Christian view of God is that God is self-giving and takes the initiative in relating to human beings by communicating through prophets and scriptures, appearing in human form in Jesus of Nazareth, and providing deliverance from the human predicament as a gift of grace. As a noted British Christian scholar observed, "Where every other religion teaches what [man] must *do*, Christianity alone tells what God has *done*."[6]

The distinguishing theological characteristic of Christianity and Christian statements about God is the person and work of Jesus Christ. This amounts to more than simple reflection upon his human life. Theologically, Jesus is said to be fully God and fully human. From the New Testament accounts,[7] Jesus, the man of Nazareth, was born supernaturally (a virginal conception), and he gradually revealed extraordinary insights into the Jewish Scriptures, displayed supernatural powers of healing and dealings with the Spirit world, and spoke of himself as having a son-ship relation to God. This last aspect Christians refer to as the incarnation ("enfleshment") of the Son of God. In the last week of his earthly life, Jesus, who had been widely acclaimed as the fulfillment of the Jewish hope for Messiah (Christ), was unjustly accused, tried, and crucified by Roman and Jewish authorities during the annual Passover celebration. Uniquely, Christians believe, Jesus was resurrected from the dead two days later through the power of God and walked about among his companions for 40 days thereafter, giving evidence of a post-Resurrection life. He then dramatically ascended into heaven from the Mount of Olives, across the Kidron Valley from Jerusalem. Christians believe he will return to that same location to establish a kingdom and consummate human history. The purpose of Jesus' life, then, became more than that of a religious martyr for his teachings and way of life, but a transmuted opportunity for human salvation and reconciliation with God. Those who accept the truthfulness of the narratives of the life of Jesus and who believe in faith in God's saving work through Christ, will inherit eternal life through his resurrection. Thus, theologically Jesus continues to be absolutely central to the meaning of Christianity and there is little unique value to Christianity without a doctrine of Christ.

Early in the evolution of Christianity, the followers of Jesus developed a sophisticated understanding of a third manifestation of God, namely the Holy Spirit. Jesus himself taught that after his earthly departure, the Spirit would reside specially in the community of believers to guide their understandings, ratify their experiences, and provide discipline for them where necessary. The New Testament book of the Acts of the Apostles is rich with instances of the direction of the Spirit, the extraordinary manifestations of the Spirit and the worship of the Spirit. This third manifestation of God, with all the attributes of the Father and the Son, emerges in the central teachings of Christianity. Taken together in the idioms of contemporary Greek culture, the creeds thus declare the Triune nature of God, or to use classic terminology, the Trinity: Father, Son, and Holy Spirit, three persons, one God. Contemporary Feminist theologians, sensitive to what appears to be patriarchal language of God, have referred to the Trinity as Creator, Redeemer, and Sustainer and are apt to speak of the Holy Spirit using feminine imagery.

The doctrine of the Trinity has other important implications for Christians. With respect to Jesus Christ, Christians believe Jesus possesses the fullness of God from eternity past. In other words, Jesus, as the Son of God, is eternal and was part of God's work in creation, for instance.[8] Some Christians are apt to interpret theophanies ("God-showings") in the Hebrew Scriptures as appearances of Christ before his earthly life.[9] During his 3-year ministry in Galilee, at least two times Jesus exhibited a superhuman persona: at his baptism by John the baptizer in the Transjordan, and later on the Mount of Transfiguration in Galilee where he appeared with the prophets Moses and Elijah. Since his ascension, Christians teach that he has joined God in the heavenly places. Likewise, the Holy Spirit is taught to be eternal and possesses all the divine nature and attributes as well. The Spirit was present at Creation, a giver of life to all humans, the reviver of the Nation Israel, an omnipresence of God, and a source of verification of the deity of Jesus Christ at his baptism. Christian scholars have long retrospectively held that the Holy Spirit appears throughout the text of the Old Testament as in King David's claim to be inspired by the Spirit of God and the prayer of Nehemiah.[10] Thus, Father, Son, and Spirit are said to be persons (*hypostases*) within a unity called the Godhead. To articulate this seeming paradox of "three-ness" yet "one-ness," two centuries of theological debate and interaction occurred (326–c.500) that culminated in the Athanasian Creed. It stated,

> For there is one Person of the Father, another of the Son, and another of the Holy Spirit.

But the Godhead of the Father, of the Son, and of the Holy Spirit is all one, the
glory equal, the majesty co-eternal.
Such as the Father is, such is the Son, and Such is the Holy Spirit.[11]

Although not a term found in Scripture, the Trinity has since the sixth century been an accepted theological reality among mainstream Christians of all denominations.[12]

Other major areas of doctrine in Christian theology are sin, humanity, salvation, last things, and the church. Christian teaching is clear about the nature of humans. Human beings are creatures of God's work in creation, created in God's image, male and female. There is a spirited debate among Christians since the nineteenth century over whether humans are an evolved species in God's creation, or a unique species created at once. Whichever position one assumes for scientific or theological reasons, the human species grew and proliferated. At a point early in their development, humans used their capacity of freedom of choice to make certain moral decisions that alienated them from God. Following Jewish theological understanding, Christians hold that humans were given the possibility of being reconciled to their Creator through an elaborate system of sacrifices that mitigated their sin. Christian theology teaches that the sacrificial system in Ancient Israel actually prefigured the work of Christ as a redeemer. In due time, Jesus became the fulfillment of a system that ultimately opened the saving work of God to all peoples. This is God's intention for all people, in order to restore God's creation. This narration of "salvation history" thus unites what God was doing for centuries in the Jewish religion, with the new understanding or covenant offered through the work of Jesus Christ. Christian theology, following Jewish thought, holds that humanity was created in God's image. This suggests from observation of human character and behavior that humans have a quality of rationality or reason, they have a moral capability called choice, and they have well-developed personalities. Humans are social beings, and capable of expressing feelings like love, hatred, affection, and sympathy. Theologians believe these characteristics are shared with God.

God's intention for humanity was to live in fellowship with a developing human species. God's order and physical creation were without blemish. At some point, however, humans rejected their creator's intention and sought to live according to their own devices. Christians call this rejection "sin" and understand that it is both a disposition or tendency, and specific acts of wrongdoing that result. Sin alienated humans from God and left them in a difficult position with respect to their sense of worth and value. Through difficult circumstances, the human race has managed to progress and prolifer-ate, subduing the planet and using its resources for their improvement and destruction. But, alienation from God continues and the greatest evidence of this reality is the limitation placed upon life. Death is inevitable: humans die, as does the rest of creation. Only through reproduction does a species continue. Thus, humans are left with the religious question of whether there is a future for humanity.

Christian theologians have wrestled with the idea of eternality or the future of humanity in several ways. The texts of the Hebrew and Christian Scriptures, written over a number of centuries and in different cultures, offer several possibilities. First, there is an expectation that some humans will achieve a righteous relationship with God and be rewarded with life after death. Another possibility is that as favored people, one ethnic group or race, such as Israel or a New Israel, will be rewarded and restored. Still another possibility is that God will select a few whom God desires to share a relation-ship with God and save them. Still another possibility for Christian theolo-gians is that God will ultimately restore everyone. The consensus over the centuries is that God wills every person to be saved, but only those who respond positively to the grace of God in Christ will be saved. Thus, a human response to God's free initiatives in Christ is part of the equation of salvation.

Several other categories of Christian doctrine from time to time help to define the Christian tradition. While the nature of the church is discussed in another context (see Chapter 2), theologically the church has special import in Christian teaching. It is understood to be of supernatural origin, chosen by God, according to Paul the Apostle "before the foundation of the world" and elsewhere referred to as "a holy and . . . royal . . . priesthood."[13] It is to be a continual witness to the work of Jesus Christ and a transformative agent in human society and a place of spiritual activity. While flawed by human error and sinfulness, "the gates of Hades will not prevail against it."[14] In the consum-mation, it will be collected together for rewards and presented to Christ (see Chapter 6).

Every major religion has some understanding of salvation or fulfillment. Christianity has a well-developed doctrine of salvation, evolved from Jewish thought and composite in nature. The history of salvation, referred to by German theologians as *heilsgeschicte*, involves ancient Hebrew understand-ings that pertain to the act of creation itself, deliverance from natural disaster, the deliverance of Israel from captivity in Egypt, then a second deliverance from exile in Babylon and in the Post-Exilic prophets, and finally, deliverance to the Kingdom of Messiah. Across the Hebrew Scriptures, the basic meaning of salvation is deliverance, and it comes to be more associated with the Nation than with individuals.

Building on that foundation, New Testament writers projected salvation into the future as a process that generally involves healing and restoration to wholeness. Salvation comes to mean a personal release from sin (deliverance), a salvation which results in eternal life. Christian theologians have developed the idea of salvation to be bound to the work of Christ who is called from his birth "savior" and only available through Christ. One is set free from the condemnation of sin in the present life, which has alienated Creator from creation; saved in the return of Christ from the judgment of God upon evil doers; and then finally saved to live eternally in God's presence. The doctrine is enriched with a multilingual vocabulary: salvation involves redemption from the bondage of sin, a Hebrew idea that relates back to servitude and the concept of a kinsman-redeemer (go'-el) that Jesus fulfills for all humanity; reconciliation in the Greek usage that involves bringing two adversarial parties together, God and humans in the God-human, Jesus; and justification, introduced by Paul from the Roman juridical context where a person is declared guilt-less by the finished work of Christ who advocates for sinners in the divine court of justice. For many Christians in the sacramental traditions, salvation is mediated only through the church and proper sacramental administration, while others would hold that salvation is automatically received upon confession of Jesus Christ as Savior and Lord which by its confession recognizes the role of Christ and the nature of salvation as a free gift, "not from works, lest anyone would boast," to use the Apostle Paul's language.[15]

In succession to the process of salvation, Christians variously understand spiritual growth for a religious person as a secondary process called sanctification. Paul wrote that Christians are new creatures in Christ, living in human, mortal bodies, but transformed in their thinking and orientation to life. Some Christians understand this to involve a second work of God in removing any hint of sinfulness at a point of consecration of oneself to God. This is often referred to as perfectionism. Others see sanctification as a lifelong process as one "surrenders" aspects of the human will over to the will and purposes of God. In Eastern Orthodoxy, this is roughly the equivalent of "theosis," or drawing into the nature and character of God. The language of holiness or heart purity is used among rigorous Christian groups to indicate how believers are expected to develop aspects of the divine character in their lives.

Another important theological category is the spirit world. Early Christians adopted a cosmology from the Jewish Scriptures that includes morally benevolent spiritual beings (angels) and malevolent beings (demons). In part, they were influenced by Persian religious thought. Angels serve God and at times the needs of humans, while the demonic spirits are under the control of a master personification of evil, variously called Satan, the Devil, Beelzebub, or the Deceiver. Through the writing of Jewish apocalyptic literature in the first and second centuries before the Christian era, and continuing into the early Christian era, characters of both sorts come through in the battles between good and evil and the playing out of human life on earth. There are archangels like Gabriel and Michael, and for some, Lucifer, who in a variant interpretation was a fallen benevolent angel of light who has metamorphosed into the Prince of Darkness. Though not supported by close textual reading, the serpent in the Genesis account of creation and the fall of humanity popularly has a persona as an early appearance of the Devil. The realm and characters of evil remain powerful foils to other teachings of salvation and Jesus Christ in classic thought.

There are important theological differences among the three major branches in the historic development of Christianity and its contemporary practice. For instance, Roman Catholic doctrine much emphasizes the grace of God through the sacraments. Protestants, however, emphasize the Christian life and the empowerment of Christian believers. Eastern Orthodox Christians blend the sacraments with a sense of communal spirituality in their unique understanding. Some have commented that the differences are so pronounced as to really indicate different religious traditions, sharing a common figure in Jesus Christ. The ecumenical movement and interreligious dialogs of the twentieth century have done much to close such theological gaps.

Many contemporary Christian theologians construct a theological narrative that covers all the religious issues of concern to humanity and reach from Genesis to Revelation, in Scripture terms. This narrative begins with the Hebrew Scriptures wherein God creates humans in the midst of a garden and places them in a probationary state. The humans fail the test and are relegated to a life of toil and eventual death. In his mercy, God designs a plan of redemption for humanity and identifies special people with whom God will act through and with. The hero is Abraham, a resident of Chaldea, who emigrated to a new location in Canaan that came to be known as the Land of Promise because of God's covenant with Abraham to bless the nations through his offspring. Abraham's family ultimately failed God and was carried off into Egypt where the children of Israel (the grandson of Abraham) were in servitude for 400 years. Moses became a second heroic figure who led God's people out of bondage and back to the Promised Land, but not before they wandered in disobedience in Sinai for 40 years. Once back in Canaan, the Israelites organized a monarchy over which the warrior king David presided, followed by his son, Solomon, an internationally oriented figure. After Solomon's reign, the kingdom divided between a northern and a southern kingdom, both of which were eventually permitted to fall under Babylonian imperialism because of their national infidelity to the true God. In Babylonian exile, the prophets of Israel foretell the restoration of Israel again to Jerusalem and the coming of Messiah or "anointed one." Israel was restored through a remnant that returned to the Land, a second temple was built and the sacrificial system was restored, although the Jewish people became a client state of other formidable empires: Greeks, Hasmoneans, Romans, etc. In the exile, the temple cult was gradually expanded to include local synagogues or worship centers throughout the Jewish world.

For Christians, the entire theological narrative reaches forward to Jesus Christ, the fulfillment of God's Anointed. Jesus appears amidst miraculous events and fits all the details of Israel's hopes. Israel, however, internally divided among competing sects, misunderstands the mission of Jesus and he is executed by the Romans. What appears to be a failed project, however, turns into a broadening redemptive mission of the resurrected Christ who is presented to the Jews first and then non-Jews as the Savior of all humanity. The church, an extension of Jesus' disciples, takes on the task of calling succeeding generations to faith in the person and work of Christ and an expectation gradually reemerges of a kingdom for Jews and non-Jews that will be established at the end of time in which the true followers of Jesus as Messiah will reign eternally with him. In the end, God defeats the powers of evil, which come to be personified in both supernatural beings and evil humans.

Although some Christians attempt to truncate the narrative by jettisoning the Jewish saga because the God of Judaism appears to be different than the God of the New Testament, or because Jews eventually rejected the deity of Jesus, the theological consensus is that only by coupling the Jewish saga with the mission of Jesus is the totality of God's intention for humanity properly understood. Jesus, a Jewish man come from God, thus restores God's primeval relationship with God's creation.

Ethics

Having established a basic Christian theological narrative, we now turn to how Christians apply what they know of God to life situations. Historically, ethics, the application of the doctrines of Christianity to practical life situations, has been a subcategory of theology. As a Christian would put it, the question of "How, then, shall we live?"[16] is of fundamental importance. Here religious texts, assertions, and principles shape the Christian life. The four Gospels indicate that Jesus spoke broadly about ethical issues, such as the use of violence and expectations of marriage and divorce. One of the defining marks of Paul the Apostle's work was moral teaching, for example, his observations to the Church at Rome in matters of human sexuality. From surviving noncanonical literature of the first through the fifth centuries, Christian communities practiced a rigorous code of conduct within their assemblies and in relation to the broader social context. St. Augustine the preeminent theologian of the first five centuries of the Christian era, wrote a definitive treatise, *On Lying*. In the Eastern Churches, Christian ethics stem from a person's growth toward being God-like or Christ-likeness (theosis) and involves both individuals and the community. One of the most important Christian thinkers to take up systematic ethical and moral concerns was Thomas Aquinas (1225–1274). Aquinas worked from an Aristotelian orientation to build a case for natural law, or the existence of immutable principles laid down in Creation by God to be the pattern by which the world and humanity should live. Aquinas' system became the bedrock of Roman Catholic teaching that expanded to include civil law and canon law (the law of the Church) as having their origins in God. Many Protestant Christians hold to the validity of a natural law as well.

During the Age of the Enlightenment, others like Immanuel Kant, Jeremy Bentham, and John Stuart Mill broadened the basis of moral decision-making and much influenced the Christian community by principles like a categorical imperative or a utilitarian system of ascertaining the greatest possible good for the most persons. In the interaction between Christian missionaries and those practicing Buddhism, Hinduism, and Confucian ethics, Christian ethics was likewise shaped by determinism, self-reflection, aspects of an afterlife, and principles of a desired moral equilibrium. Pertinent to Christian ethics are questions of just war, right to life, responsible use of the earth's resources, sexuality, gender, race/ethnicity, religious freedom, and world order, to mention the major categories.

Beginning in the twentieth century with theologians like Karl Barth, Walter Raushenbusch, and Reinhold Niebuhr, Christian ethics has developed into a major category of Christian theology. Since the 1950s, with the work of Paul Lehman, Joseph Fletcher, James Gustafson, Helmut Thielicke, and Stanley Hauerwas, Christian ethics has become a discourse in its own right. Christian ethicists follow patterns like those who understand duty or rules to guide the Christian life, like the Ten Commandments or the Beatitudes (deontological ethics), while others look to the results of one's action or position (teleological ethics), or through a thorough analysis of a given situation (situation ethics).

The history of militarism from the nineteenth and twentieth centuries and Christian complicity in international conflicts has caused serious reflection and debate across the Christian community about a Christian position on war and military service. For centuries, from St. Augustine through Thomas Aquinas, the Catholic and Orthodox Churches have defended a theory of just war. The foundations of this position are that the war must have a just cause, the military conduct must follow accepted rules and avoid (if possible) the harming of noncombatants, and there must be a reasonable expectation of victory. Such ethical discourse was seen in the rationale for the Crusades and subsequent wars in Europe and the colonial era. A crisis occurred, however, when Christian powers fought against each other in the First World War and weapons of mass destruction were employed in the Second World War. Major theological voices were raised on both sides of the question, for instance, Reinhold Niebuhr who argued for a just war position in observing that "a responsible relationship to the political order makes an unqualified disavowal of violence impossible because there will always be crises in which the cause of justice will have to be defended against those who will attempt its violent destruction,"[17] and later Harry Emerson Fosdick and Martin Luther King, Jr. who questioned the legitimacy of war in resolving conflict. Among the most important Christian voices advocating a pacifist position was John Howard Yoder, a Mennonite. Yoder, in a widely acclaimed essay, asserted in 1971, ". . . every member of the Body of Christ is called to absolute non-resistance in discipleship."[18] There is mixed opinion among Christians as to whether violence [war] is ever justified.

The advent of environmental concerns and advances in medical technology has led the Christian community to consider how to apply the teachings of Scripture and a theistic orientation to serious social issues. For instance, the extreme deforestation of large parts of the world's ecosystems led to a new call for becoming stewards of the earth, turning back centuries of exploitation of natural resources under a dominion idea derived from Genesis 1.28 of using the environment for human needs. This has been further hastened by the evidence in favor of global warming that began with the scientific community and was carried forth in the last decade by U.S. Vice President Albert Gore (a Baptist Christian),[19] and now widely accepted among both the mainstream Protestant and evangelical Christian churches. Increasing numbers of Christians in Europe and North America have adopted a theocentric ethics that sees intrinsic value in all of creation and not just for the pleasure and profit of humanity. Process theologians like John Cobb have long emphasized the interdependence of the biosphere and have called for an ecological ethic.[20] Jürgen Moltmann, a leading Reformed theologian who is convinced that a deadly ecological crisis has emerged, has observed, "An ecological doctrine of creation implies a new kind of thinking about God . . . the centre of this thinking is the recognition of the presence of God in the world and the presence of the world in God."[21] Medical technology that has introduced procedures that clone animals and human beings, in an attempt to reverse infertility, and map gene codes for diseases and conditions, has prompted vigorous debates. The Catholic Church has revisited its historic position on birth control, evangelicals have dismissed cloning and euthanasia, and the genome project has advocates on both sides who see the value of combating serious health conditions, with some critics worrying about modifications to natural life cycles and processes.

Another area of ethical inquiry in which Christians have distinguished themselves is human rights. Plainly, Jesus taught dignity for all persons, the value of work and education, the right of free religious inquiry, the right to move from one place to another. Importantly, he treated women in his circle of friends and adherents with respect uncommon for his era. The Apostle Paul wrote of spiritual freedom, while he also countenanced slavery and the dominance of males over females in certain Christian assemblies.[22] Yet, Christian history is replete with chapters of bigotry against Jews and Muslims, and dominance over other world religions, plus giving support to slavery and persecution of nonbelievers. Martin Luther provides one of the darkest profiles with respect to anti-Semitic attitudes and practices and those in the Dutch and English slave trade for over 300 years were often leaders in the advancement of Christian civilization.

One can make a strong case, however, for Christian understanding of and support for human rights. Samuel Wesley, Sr. and his illustrious son, John Wesley, charted a new course in opposing the slave trade and the institution of slavery itself. The Quakers, who live on the margins of institutional Christianity, opposed slavery and upheld the rights of women from the eighteenth century. In the United States and England, during the first half of the nineteenth century, the Protestant churches began to pursue various efforts in human rights, including abolition, initiatives toward peace, universal education, and women's rights. In the United States, these positions often deeply divided their constituencies for decades. With the outbreak of the First World War where the great powers of Europe (which happened to be the leading Christian nations also) attempted to dominate each other, the Christian community developed a global consciousness that led to solid participation in a human rights movement. Following the lead of two Christian U.S. presidents and a prominent spouse, Woodrow Wilson and Franklin and Eleanor Roosevelt, and Sir Winston Churchill in Britain, western Christian nations embraced principles of self-determination and religious freedom. After the Second World War, Mrs. Roosevelt became the chief architect of the Universal Declaration of Human Rights, ratified by the United Nations General Assembly in 1948. Help in this achievement came through the behind-the-scenes work of Christian statesmen like John Humphrey of Canada and Charles Malik, a Lebanese Reformed Church Christian, trained at Harvard under Alfred North Whitehead. While timid at first, the various branches of the Christian family in succession joined the human rights chorus through the work of the World Council of Churches (WCC) that produced its own statement, "A Declaration on Religious Liberty" in 1948,[23] Pope John XXIII's *Pacem in Terris* in 1961, the Vatican II Council of the Roman Catholic Church in 1963–1965 in which Pope Paul VI promulgated *Dignitatis Humanae,* and still later the Lausanne (1974) and Manila (1989) declarations of the international evangelical communities. In recent years Christians have reached consensus on ethical concerns such as the dignity of all persons created in the image of God, religious freedom without qualification, the right to food, shelter, and education, a universal support for justice, and nonviolence in arbitrating disputes.

In summary

The study of religion is a quest for ultimate answers concerning life and self. Christianity has a well developed, thoroughly debated response to the ultimate questions and an orientation to enjoy life to its fullest. Christian theology contains several categories of assertions about God, salvation, and humanity. As a text-based religion, Christianity is boundaried by its Scriptures, the Old and New Testaments. Christian theologians work with natural truth that is derived from human experience and ratified in tradition, as well as revealed truth that is recorded in the Scriptures as a unique form of communication from God. A significant difference of opinion exists over the relative authority of texts that were written over several centuries and over those included in the approved books of Scripture. Another area of debate is whether God continues to reveal truth through present experience. And finally, there is the question of whether Christianity is an exclusive theological pathway.

In addition to the system of doctrines that constitute theology in an historical and biblical sense, Christians are concerned to be faithful to the mission of Christ in building his Kingdom and transforming the world. The field of ethics has grown from a theological category to become the application of the teachings of Jesus and the apostles to a wide variety of life issues. These include the dignity of human life, gender and race relations, the environment, peace and justice, and human rights. There may be great latitude and debate over specific stances Christians are expected to assume, but there is no doubt that there is a correlation between theology and life. Millions of Christians over twenty centuries have been transformed by the ideals and principles of Christianity.

For further reading and study

Anderson, J. N. D., editor, *The World's Religions*. Grand Rapids, MI: William B. Eerdmans Publishing Co., 1968.

Aquinas, Thomas. "Fruition of Natural Desire in the Beatific Vision," *Compendium of Theology*. Translated by Cyril Vollert. London: B. Herder, 1948. Barth, Karl. *Church Dogmatics*. 13 vols. Edinburgh: T&T Clark, 1955.

Brunner, Emil. *Dogmatics*. London: Lutterworth Press, 1949.

Cobb, John B. Jr. *Process Theology: An Introductory Exposition*. Louisville, KY: Westminster John Knox Press, 1976.

Dunn, James D. G. *The Theology of the Apostle Paul*. Grand Rapids, MI: Eerdmans, 1998.

Ehrman, Bart D. *The New Testament: An Historical Introduction to the Early Christian Writings Third Edition*. New York: Oxford University Press, 2004.

Gustafson, James. *Theology and Christian Ethics*. Philadelphia, PA: United Church Press, 1974.

Hauwerwas, Stanley, and Willimon, William. *Resident Aliens: Life in the Christian Colony*. Nashville, TN: Abingdon Press, 1989.

Küng, Hans. *Theology for the Third Millennium: An Ecumenical View*. New York: Doubleday Publishers, 1988.

Lewis, C. S. *Mere Christianity*. San Francisco, CA: Harper, 2001.

Migliore, Daniel. *Faith Seeking Understanding. An Introduction to Christian Theology*. Grand Rapids, MI: Eerdmans, 1991.

Moltmann, Jürgen. *God in Creation: A New Theology of Creation and the Spirit of God*. San Francisco, CA: Harper & Row, 1985.

Niebuhr, H. Richard. *Christ and Culture*. New York: Harper Brothers, 1951.

Niebuhr, Reinhold. *An Interpretation of Christian Ethics*. New York: Harper Brothers, 1935.

Pannenburg, Wolfhart. *Systematic Theology*. 3 vols. Grand Rapids, MI: Eerdmans, 1991–1998.

Tillich, Paul. *The Protestant Era*. Chicago, IL: University of Chicago Press, 1948.

Smith, Wilfred Cantwell. *Towards a World Theology: Faith and the Comparative History of Religion*. Philadelphia, PA: The Westminster Press, 1981.

Thielicke, Helmut. *Theological Ethics*. Grand Rapids, MI: Eerdmans, 1979.

Tillich, Paul. *Systematic Theology*. Chicago, IL: University of Chicago Press, 1951.

Yoder, John Howard. "Peace Without Eschatology" in *The Original Revolution: Essays in Christian Pacifism*. Scottdale, PA: Herald Press, 1971.

Yoder, John Howard. *The Politics of Jesus*. Second Edition. Grand Rapids, MI: Eerdmans, 1994.

4 Christian Spirituality

Christian spirituality refers to the psychological or experiential dimensions of Christian faith and life, a combination of piety, devotion, prayer, and contemplation, a kind of quest for meaning in Christ.[1] Spirituality is distinct from dogma or beliefs, and typically involves rituals, symbols, and sensory experiences that are given religious meaning, like the recitation of a sacred text, the presence of a cross, or an act of cleansing in water. From individual and community perspectives, Christians use the vocabulary of prayer, worship, and devotion. Christian spiritual directors are keenly aware of the importance of ritual, symbol, prayer, and discipline. Our discussion will follow these patterns.

Ritual in religious contexts is defined as acts or routines that express anxiety before that which is sacred. Some rituals display a desire for communion with divine beings, a fear of punishment, a need for purification, expectancy, a celebration, a change of status, or recognition of rites of passage.[2] The theory of W. Robertson Smith, with respect to the relationship of ritual to belief, applies to the Christian tradition: "Religion in primitive times was not a system of belief with practical applications; it was a body of fixed traditional practices, to which every member of the society conformed as a matter of course."[3] In the case of primitive Christianity, emerging from within Judaism, ritual or praxis appears to have preceded systematic dogma or belief.

Christianity exhibits a wide variety of ritual expression and acts of devotion and discipline. Some Christian ritual is captured under the heading of worship, while other acts are spiritual disciplines or personal devotions. The Christian religion over time and in various cultures is sufficiently diverse to produce differing emphases or priorities in rituals. For instance, at the heart of the Orthodox tradition is *prayer*. For Roman Catholics, the idea of *sacrament* is fundamental to Christian ritual. For Protestants, the sacramental principle has been modified and reduced to conform to the practices of the early churches of the New Testament era. Protestants thus stress individual prayers, devotions, and study of sacred texts. Christians do practice communion with God, they do fear God in the sense of reverent worship, and Christians do celebrate changes in personal status and rites of passage. Less common among Christians are acts of expectancy, but dietary observances and wearing and use of sacral jewelry fall into this category.

Variously interpreted, at the core of Christian ritual, worship, and devotion is the teaching of John 4.23: "True worshippers shall worship the Father in Spirit and in truth; for the Father seeks such to worship Him." There are two levels involved in ritual, the material or behavioral, and the spiritual, which for Christians is a way of expressing the attitudinal or personal aspects. While Christians generally understand the need in Ancient Israel for the various prescribed rituals of tabernacle, temple, and synagogue, they separate the material from the spiritual. In the tradition of the prophets, Christians learn from the Hebrew Scriptures that God came to despise feast days; God took no delight in solemn assemblies, and did not accept burnt offerings from the unrighteous.[4] Rather, as Israelite King David in an earlier generation learned, "the sacrifices acceptable to God are a broken spirit and a contrite heart."[5] From Jesus' experience, Christians heard his words about the Temple: "Is it not written, My house shall be called of all nations the house of prayer? But you have made it a den of thieves."[6] Yet, the power and efficacy of Christian ritual is not lost in the ultimate beatific vision:

> The four living creatures did not rest day or night, saying, Holy, holy, holy, Lord
> God Almighty, who was, and is, and is to come . . . the four and twenty elders fall
> down before him that is seated on the throne and worship him that lives forever

and ever and cast their crowns before the throne, saying, You are worthy, O Lord, to receive glory and honor and power . . .[7]

A modern Christian theologian, Geoffrey Wainwright, has observed, "the second-order activity of theology is . . . properly doxological," that is, at a fundamental level, worship is communion with God: a conversation with God, a participation in the character and nature of God, an enjoyment of the presence of God in one's life.[8] To be doxological is to be praising God in response to God's character and God's works. In the Christian experience that is accomplished through ritual and liturgy and these elements are of utmost importance to the religious tradition.

A Christian understanding of prayer

In general, prayer has been defined as a verbal ritual that seeks to exert a favorable influence upon spiritual powers, petitionary in nature rather than coercive.[9] Prayer is a fundamental aspect of Christian experience and it relates both to practice and theology. Christian prayer does not assume that humans must apply to a disinterested deity for all good things, but rather depicts a parent who freely bestows goodness out of love. Christians do not share the uncertainty of other religions in petitioning deity or a lack of confidence in the outcome of prayer. Christians are enjoined to have a "right attitude" in prayer.[10]

Christians share with historic Judaism a common foundational understanding of prayer. In Jesus' era, Jewish prayer involved a physical bowing or kneeling that spoke of submission and acknowledgment of God's sovereignty. Directions were important also: prayer was directed upwards toward heaven and often hands were outstretched upwards. Praying toward the east was likewise important because the Mount of Olives, the scene of Jesus' departure to heaven and his anticipated return, was to the east. Like other religions, Jesus' prayers involved preparation for special emphasis or intensity. Fasting before prayer brought about a concentration and inward focus.

Following the teachings of Jesus, Christians think of God as personal and thus God may be addressed by name. Sometimes the prayer is addressed to God as creator, but more often to Jesus Christ, the Risen Lord. Individuals pray and believe that God responds to them, or "answers" prayers. Prayer is a conversation that bridges the human and divine spheres. Answers to prayers come in many forms: an existential answer may be received by an individual who is convinced of a course of action or a reason why something has not transpired, for which they have prayed earnestly. Another answer to prayers may come through an intermediary person. A next of kin or other Christian person may give a word of knowledge that speaks directly to a person's prayer. Yet another possibility of answered prayer is through a reading of Scripture in which God may use the written words of a passage to communicate to a contemporary need or question. Still others find that prayers are answered by the medium of a prophet or preacher who may not even be aware that their words are reaching individuals. Christians therefore must exercise both constant sensitivity to how God will answer prayer and discernment about the answers should be in keeping with knowledge of God in Scripture and human experiences. This much Christians share with their Jewish brothers and sisters.

Jesus of Nazareth, however, introduced a new dimension to prayer that was taken up by his disciples and became a canon of the Christian community. He urged through a patterned prayer called commonly "The Lord's Prayer," an affectionate, familial addressing of God as "Father" or literally, "Daddy." This was meant to be the expression of a devoted son or daughter, in the case of Jesus, as God's only beloved Son. Jesus urged his followers first to bless or enlarge the name of God; then, request forgiveness of their sins. His prayer presented individual needs and resolved that the end of all prayer was a hope that the Kingdom of God would be established through God's sovereignty. Significantly, Jesus also raised expectations for his disciples about the outcomes of prayer. He said, "All things you shall ask in prayer, believing, you shall receive" (Matthew 21.22). And, elsewhere in his famous Sermon on the Mount, Jesus taught, "Ask and you shall receive; seek and you shall find; knock, and it shall be opened to you. For everyone that asks, receives . . ."[11]

Prayer in the Christian tradition makes three assumptions about the Christian theological understanding of God. First, that God is aware of and concerned about human circumstances. Christians believe that God superintends what happens in all of God's domain and that nothing falls outside God's capability to administrate. Through the doctrine of the Holy Spirit, God is present (the theological term is "immanent") in the very essence of nature and influencing human behavior and events and circumstances. Second, prayer assumes that God may be disposed to modify his response to human needs. If God had a preordered design on events or upon a person, God's response to prayer may modify the outcome God had originally intended or planned to allow. Petitioning a disinterested or uniformed deity would produce no recognizable results that could be attributed to the deity: this was the Apostle Paul's response to those worshipping several deities on Mars Hill when he visited Athens. Through parable stories that Jesus taught, Christians are enjoined to be persistent in prayer to impress upon God the urgency and sincerity of their needs and queries. And third, prayer assumes that God responds to human articulations based on their faithfulness to God's laws: "The effective, fervent prayer of a righteous man avails much," to quote a proverb used in the early Christian community at Jerusalem.[12]

As we have seen, Christian prayers are uttered most often in the name of Christ. Jesus told his disciples to baptize in his name, to preach and heal in his name, and to bring their petitions to God in his name: "Whatever you ask in my name, that will I do . . . If you shall ask anything in my name, I will do it."[13] Theologically, Jesus as the Son of God has access to his Heavenly Father and provides that same access to his disciples. The writer of the New Testament Epistle to the Hebrews put it this way: "For Christ has not entered the holy places made with hands . . . but into heaven itself, now to appear in the presence of God for us . . ."[14] Christians refer to this work of Christ as his high priestly ministry on behalf of Christian believers. Thus, it is common for Christians to conclude their prayers with words like "in the name of Jesus Christ, Savior and Lord, Amen."

Paul, the great apostle and interpreter of the teachings of Jesus, believed wholeheartedly in prayer. For him prayer was the essence of a daily spirituality: "Pray without ceasing," he wrote to the Christians at Thessalonika.[15] In Paul's experience, prayer served several purposes, including intercession for the needs of leaders and those in the local assemblies, requests for unusual divine interventions (as with the Apostle Peter's imprisonment), prayer as worship, spiritual communion with God, a demonstration of sincerity and empathy with crisis situations, and as a special linguistic liturgical device (glossolalia = speaking in tongues).

Virtually all Christian denominations practice some form of communal prayers. The "Lord's Prayer" was intended to be a community prayer and Jesus evidently intended that his disciples would pray with him.[16] Communal prayers may be invocative, thanksgiving, or intercessory. Since the effectiveness of prayer is related to the special qualities of the intercessor, this can be compounded in community prayers as many "righteous" pray. In many congregations, a priest or pastor offers weekly prayers for the people of the congregation. This may involve a litany wherein the priest makes certain declarations, usually in the style of biblical language and metaphors, with similar responses from the congregants. Communal prayers mirror the practice of the early churches, which were described as "continuing with one accord in prayer and supplication."[17] Contemporary evangelical Christians engage in communal prayers because they hold that collectively the influence of their supplications increases as with the case of the Apostle Peter who was incarcerated by Herod in Jerusalem (Acts 12.5). Christians continue to believe that this kind of prayer practice produces spiritual fervency and heightens expectations.[18]

Liturgical prayers constitute an important kind of spiritual device for many Christians. Written by various pious persons in the Christian community—Augustine, Gregory, Hildegard, Luther, Cranmer—liturgical prayers are syntheses of Scripture and embellished phraseology that are used in collective and individual worship. They express for the many and across time the depths of one's devotion and needs. Typical is the "Great Confession" attributed to Thomas Cranmer, Archbishop of Canterbury:

> Almighty and most merciful God, we have erred and strayed from Thy ways like lost sheep. We have followed too much the devices and desires of our own hearts. We have offended against Thy holy laws. We have left undone those things which we ought to have done; and we have done those things which we ought not to have done. Spare Thou those who confess their faults. Restore Thou those who are penitent, according to Thy promises declared unto mankind in Christ Jesus our Lord. And grant, O most merciful Father, for His sake, that we may ever hereafter live a godly, righteous and sober life, to the glory of thy Holy Name. Amen.[19]

Some Christians believe that liturgical prayers can become dull and rote, less than personal expressions. Consequently, extemporaneous prayers are often given as free-flowing, voluntary, personal outpourings of devotion. Generally exhibited in the Free Churches, the pattern and structure of extemporaneous prayers must be learned. The Lord's Prayer and other biblical examples create the patterns with circumstances and petitions contemporary to the supplicant, filling in the appropriate spaces in the pattern. Often, particular leaders can be thought to have the gift of oral expression in prayer and can provide individually that collective vocalization for a congregation.

The special use of iconography in prayer in the Eastern Christian tradition is more than artwork. Icons, as images of Christ and the Saints, create a context or a "tabernacle" in which Christian faith can be expressed in images as well as words. In praying before icons, Orthodox worshippers receive divine grace and holiness that the subject of the icon carries. John of Damascus, a seventh- to eighth-century Eastern theologian, taught that the grace attained by the saints in their lives continues to dwell in their images and can be conveyed to worshippers who are changed by the likenesses of the saints. Icons continue to enrich the devotional life of Greek and Russian churches, plus a rising number of Protestant believers.

One of the remarkable aspects of the Christian spirituality of prayer in both ancient times and more modern eras has been the "season of prayer." Originally known as "nights of prayer," these are extended periods—several days or even weeks—devoted singularly to prayer. For Paul the apostle, the purpose of these extended prayers was to bring before God the concerns of the whole congregation and all the churches as well as of the missionary outreach in which he was engaged. He urged various churches in his circle to "continue steadfastly in prayer, being watchful in it."[20] In the Pastoral Letters, this was the work of widows who held prayer vigils. In the contemporary churches, seasons of prayer can be held during periods of the Christian calendar, such as Lent, and in response to a specific crisis like the illness of a leader or a natural disaster.

A Christian understanding of prayer must always involve an element of mystery. The question of why God should answer some prayers and not all, or some in the affirmative and others in the negative, troubles many believers. Theologians respond by asserting the prerogatives of God's nature and that ultimately God's will is benevolent. The response of last resort is ignorance of the complete will and purposes of God.

Ritual and worship in the early churches

Worship and ritual in early Christianity were influenced by culture and tradition. Applied generally to all religions, "worship" means the ascription of value or worth to a deity. As we have noted, Jewish worship involved a "bowing down" in honor of God, as well as a sense of service to God. Christian worship incorporated both of these ideas into its character. Jesus of Nazareth, the founder, recognized the values of the Jewish tradition in worship, but he would not be bound by them.[21] Instead, in his adult ministry he appeared in the Temple and synagogues to proclaim his message and to do things differently. He healed on the Sabbath, he broke down the distinctions between the sacred and the profane, and he placed little emphasis upon the feasts in Israel's religious life. He was a person of almost continual prayer. Christian commentator Ferdinand Hahn suggested that the primary differences in Jesus' pattern of worship were that he moved away from ritualization and legalism and he set aside the Temple cult.[22]

Christian worship after Jesus became highly differentiated. Several writers have observed that Christianity was characterized by an exclusivistic style and meaning of worship. While God expected all persons to bow before him, he did not tolerate other deities in worship acts. Paul, for instance, instructed the Corinthian believers to put aside their pagan activities (I Cor. 8, 10). Somewhat strangely in the Roman world, there were no Christian shrines, no physical Christian Temple, no cultic priesthood, and no Christian public displays in the first century. Instead, New Testament scholar Larry Hurtado has found that early Christian worship featured intimacy, participation, fervor, and potency, among other characteristics. Worship was significant in the life of the community, as the writer to the Hebrews suggested, "Forsake not the assembling of ourselves together . . . but exhorting one another . . ."[23] The term *kyriakos,* used to denote the Lord's Supper and the Lord's Day, brought official significance to the worshipping communities.[24]

A reading of the diversity of cultures and styles and leadership among the early churches suggests that worship and ritual were simplistic, centered on Christ, and much influenced by Jewish forms boundaried by the Law, Hellenistic Jewish freedom from the Law, and Gentile needs. Palestinian Aramaic-speaking Jews doubtless wanted to return to the Law. Yet in Antioch, a Greek version of the Scriptures was used and Temple worship was spiritualized. Individual Christians were of greater importance. Different altogether, Gentiles were much given to life in the Spirit and sought the use of spiritual gifts. Christian worship was therefore inclined to the type of community that shaped it.

A simple Christian worship experience would have been a service of 2–3 hours duration that included the following rituals: prayers, the reading of Old Testament Scriptures, the sharing of narratives from the life of Christ, reading of correspondence from the apostles, a collection for the needs of the community, and singing of hymns, and gospel songs. Doubtless, the canonical Scriptures of Christianity emerged from the needs and desires of the worshipping communities. Collectively, these rituals came to be known as "liturgy," or a form or pattern.

Two specific ritual observances were present from the beginning in the primitive Christian communities, both enjoined by Jesus. The first was a celebration of the Lord's Supper. This simple sharing of the elements of bread and wine was of huge symbolic significance to true disciples, a kind of solidarity ritual.[25] It was a nuanced version of the Passover Meal that Jesus had introduced new meaning at his last observation with his inner circle. He had spoken of himself as the bread of life and the wine came to represent the blood of a new covenant that was ratified in his sacrifice on the cross. As in the Old Testament usages (see Leviticus chs. 1–7) his self-sacrifice would atone for the sins of many and he asked each of his disciples to drink of the common cup of wine signifying their identification with his sacrifice. The Gospels indicate that Jesus intended the inner circle to pass along this new ritual supper to succeeding generations as a commemoration of his work and sacrifice. This happened in the new communities and the newly converted Paul even gave specific instructions about how he believed Christ had instructed him to administer the Supper among the Corinthian believers.

The second major ritual of the primitive Christian community was baptism. It had a rich set of meanings from Hebrew usage that ran from a cleansing rite to an act of initiation in the Qumran community. For Christians, they could recall Jesus' own submission to the baptism of his cousin, John, at Bethany-beyond-Jordan. Further, two gospel writers recalled his commission to recruit new followers by initiating them through baptism.[26] Then there was the teaching of Paul to the Church at Rome that baptism was in a mystical way a symbolic ritual that experientially depicted the death, burial, and resurrection of Jesus. Baptism thus became obligatory in the life of the churches and the pilgrimage of individual Christian believers.

Other minor ritualistic practices came about as well, all grounded in the practices of the early churches. Next to baptism and the Lord's Supper was the practice of the laying on of hands. In Mark's gospel it was the means of healing the sick; when multiple elders participate, it can be a collective invocation of the blessing of God. In the earliest decades of the Church, the coming of the Spirit was associated with the laying on of hands.[27] Later, according to the epistles it was done to commission or set apart persons for a task. Another ritual was the washing of feet as Jesus did for his disciples to teach the concept of servant-hood. Some primitive churches greeted each other with the kiss of peace, also known as the kiss of charity; a contemporary Protestant version of the greeting is the "right hand of fellowship" given to new members when they are received into a congregation. At the community level, early Christians practiced fellowship rituals at important rites of passage like funerals and weddings. As early church historian Wayne Meeks has suggested, the Apostle

Paul's phrase, "in the Lord" may have been a clue as to prevailing relational or celebrative rituals that originated in the first century.[28]

A barely noticed ancient aspect of ritual is the nomenclature of address among Christians. All Christians are considered to be a family or "Body of Christ." Men and women, therefore, are "brothers" and "sisters" in Christ. These titles have been used in addressing each other across the centuries. For those in leadership, the term "elder" has been borrowed and by the seventeenth century among Protestants, the adjective "reverend" was in use. Among Church of England and Roman Catholic clergy, for those in superior positions, it is customary to refer to leaders as the "Right Reverend," the "Very Reverend," etc. Such practices are a kind of quasi-ritual within the communities of faith.

The sacraments or ordinances

Early in the development of the Christian tradition, a sophisticated understanding of spirituality became evident. As sacred rituals emerged, other sacred acts or sacraments evolved. The term *sacrament* (Gr. *mysterion*) is not found in the biblical text, yet the idea of sacraments is a derivation of centuries of Christian reflection. The word means "mystery" and is cradled in the notion that human beings cannot know in material terms the grace of God, which is a spiritual reality. Thus, a sign is needed that testifies to God's work. God has given the church such signs in Scripture and these relate directly to the person and work of Christ. Sacraments are carried on within the church; they are not individualistic. For many Christians the sacraments are the principal way of ministering to people and sustaining their religious life.[29] The Orthodox Churches and the Roman Catholic Church share an ancient tradition of 6–7 sacraments or "holy mysteries" as the Orthodox call them. The Church of England, the Lutheran Churches, Presbyterians, and other smaller Protestant bodies also use the terminology "sacrament," but define it differently, using words like "promise," "badge," or "testament."[30] Ecumenical Christianity is generally comfortable with sacramental terminology.[31]

Even a casual reading of the passages relating to the Lord's Supper demonstrates that there was a deeper meaning involved than a fellowship meal among Jesus and his colleagues. He gave new spiritual meaning to commonplace elements of bread and wine. Thus, when St. Paul later gave instructions for celebration of the Supper to the Christians at Corinth, he followed Jesus' lead in instituting a sign that pointed to a reality of Christ: "As often as you eat this bread and drink this cup, you show forth the Lord's death until he returns."[32] Likewise, baptism became a sign of the death, burial, and resurrection of Christ, in which believers may share. To those in the primitive churches, these two rites seemed plain enough in their institution and recognition by Jesus and their pointing specially to aspects of his life and teachings.

The idea of formal rites with theological meanings took root in the first two centuries of Christian development. St. Augustine, in many ways the author of the Roman Catholic understanding of these rites, wrote of sacraments that they were the visible words of God: "words added to elements like water to signify invisible realities."[33] In the sixth century CE, Gregory the Great, who created an authoritative version for the celebration of the sacrament of the Eucharist, said, "the Sacrifice of the holy altar, when offered with tears and kindliness of heart, contributes peculiarly to one's absolution [from sin]."[34] Peter Lombard, a twelfth-century medieval teacher of theology at Paris, is credited with establishing the number of sacraments at seven, though this was not officially proclaimed until the Council of Florence in 1439.

With elaborate theological underpinning, **baptism** became an initiatory rite, derived from earlier religious practices among the Hebrew sects. It signifies cleansing and purification, it portrays the gospel as in Paul's teachings (Romans 6.1–2), and it is an act of obedience to the command and practice of Jesus. Applied to infants, baptism is thought to remove the stain of inherited sin, which would prevent the soul of a newborn from entering the Kingdom of Heaven. In general, baptism brings remission of sins, an infusion of grace into a believer, and incorporation into the Church. In this regard, some early theologians, notably Augustine, held that a desire to be baptized and martyrdom were equivalents to actual baptism. The mode of baptism in the primitive churches as well as Eastern Orthodoxy, is immersion, while sprinkling or aspersion has been the practice in Western Christianity. Groups like the Baptists and evangelical sects have revived the practice of believer's or adult baptism by immersion.

In the Roman and Orthodox traditions, **confirmation** is an important next step either with or following baptism. It marks the grace of the Holy Spirit upon a baptized person and indicates removal of sin, admission to the Church, a "sealing" to eternal life, and the gift of the Spirit. In some instances confirmation, or Chrismation (the Eastern Orthodox usage), comes at the time of baptism, while in others it can be separated for convenience and spiritual maturity. Among Roman Catholics, the typical age is seven, though adults can be confirmed as well. Anglicans, Lutherans, Presbyterians, and Methodists all practice some form of confirmation, but do not hold it as a sacrament. In Catholic practice, bishops, in their capacity as teachers, retained the rite of confirmation to insure the candidate's grasp of the Christian faith, but this has largely been delegated to parish priests when a bishop is not available. In Eastern Orthodox practice, the oil of myrrh is used on all parts of a person's body and a candidate's hair is cut (or tonsured) in the shape of a cross to demonstrate a complete offering of oneself to God.

The issue of sins committed after baptism and confirmation has led Christians to another sacrament, **penance**. Penance involves confession, contrition, and absolution. Penance became in the Middle Ages an elaborate process in which manuals categorizing sins were employed and degrees of punishment were meted out in light of particular sins. Penitential acts included fasting, continence, pilgrimages, and imprisonment. After Vatican II (1963) in the Roman Catholic Church, stress was placed upon reconciliation, prayer, scripture reading, and private confession. Notably among Protestants, the Church of England practices a non-sacramental rite of penance. Other churches urge repentance and confession at the time of Holy Communion.

At the heart of Christian sacramental observances is the **Eucharist,** also called the Mass, Holy Communion, the Lord's Supper, and among the Eastern Orthodox Churches, the Divine Liturgy. At the base of the Eucharist is the principle of thanksgiving, which either refers to Jesus' words of institution, "giving thanks," or because this central act of Christian worship is a supreme act of thanksgiving in itself. The Eucharist brings to the Christian believer the elements of bread and wine that represent the body and blood of Jesus. Upon eating the bread and drinking the wine, the person's sins are remitted or forgiven (Matthew 26.28) as the symbol conveys the actual sacrifice of Christ on the cross where his body was broken and his blood was shed for the sins of the world. Orthodox Christians uphold the communal import of the Eucharist as an "all-embracing act of Holy Communion of many persons having the same faith, the same hope, the same baptism . . ., living and dead, all of the members of the Orthodox faith.[35] While the sacrament may be offered individually to the sick in the Roman Catholic tradition, in the Eastern rite, it is never given privately by the clergy alone, always understood as "on behalf of all and for all." While Reformers of the sixteenth century and others have debated whether the bread and wine are symbols or transformed substances, the vast majority of all Christians from the first century have given the Eucharist the highest priority of all sacraments. It is celebrated frequently and usually by a qualified priest or elder. The two major branches of Christianity plus many Protestant groups reserve actual reception of the sacrament or ordinance to those who are fully committed to the teachings of the Churches. This is frequently called "close[d] communion."

Roman Catholics continue to hold to three additional sacraments, Holy Orders, Marriage, and Extreme Unction. **Holy orders** or ordination can be traced back to Christ's commissioning of his disciples; The Council of Trent first declared Orders as a sacrament in 1565 because the Church taught that, like baptism, Holy Orders impart an indelible character on the person becoming a priest. In **marriage**, the sacramental dimension devolved from Aquinas and others who declared that marriage conferred grace and signified God's blessing upon the couple. The Eastern Churches have not always considered marriage sacramental and most other Christian churches have denied any sacramental aspect. Similarly in the Eastern Churches, Holy Orders is not articulated as a sacrament in quite the same way as in the West, but the ordained priesthood does guarantee the mystical life of the Church through the presence of Christ. **Extreme Unction**, or the anointing of the sick or dying, is sacramental as a final rite preparatory to death. In recent years, with the possible restoration to health of the sick person, unction has become a prayer and anointing of the sick and allowable more than once. Eastern Orthodox Christians emphasize the return of a person to his/her creator in the midst of the Church's prayers and intercessions. Anointing is practiced in both the Eastern and Roman Churches at baptism and confirmation.

Across the various streams of the sixteenth century, Reformation debate arose about the number and meaning of the sacraments. Generally, the Protestant churches reduced the number from seven to two, baptism and the Lord's Supper or Communion. Unsure of the final essence of the bread and wine in the Eucharist, Wycliffe, Luther, and Calvin denied transubstantiation. Stress was laid upon the spiritual aspects of the sacraments within the experience of the individual, rather than upon form or matter of the sacramental act. Radical reformers like Anabaptists and later Baptists and evangelicals, dropped the terminology of sacraments and took up the symbolic language of "ordinances," by which they emphasized obedience to Christ's two instructions. Certain groups like the Quakers and Salvation Army do not allow for sacraments or ordinances at all. In recent decades, among Roman Catholics there is a tendency to avoid mechanical explanations of the sacraments in favor of the enhanced use of Scripture in the observances and stress upon the faithfulness of Christ over liturgical rules or the fitness of a priest.

Various Christian groups also practice sacred acts and rituals that are less than sacramental. Catholic Christians for instance, perform 'sacramental acts' like blessing baptismal water, dedicating a church, exchanging rings in marriage, praying in the name of the Blessed Virgin Mary, exorcism, and giving the sign of the cross, while Protestants return thanks at a meal or give a 'right hand of fellowship' upon receiving a new member of a congregation.

The Christian year

The evolution of an annual cycle of feasts and rituals is an important development in Christian heritage that facilitates the rituals and sacraments. Originally, there was an obvious transfer from Israelite feasts like the Feast of Weeks or Passover to Pentecost and the Lord's Supper, respectively.[36] There were also recastings of Roman and Barbarian feasts or celebrations like Solis Invicti and Yuletide that became Christmas, and Lupercalia that presages the Easter season.[37]

By the fifth century CE the leaders of the Christian Church began to organize a formal series of events that became a Christian annual cycle or year. It was drawn from the Christian scriptures, especially the Gospels. In the West, the cycle began in the late autumn with **Advent,** which recognized the coming of Christ, especially the birth stories. At the heart of Advent is the birth of Christ, which, though it likely occurred in the winter months, was moved to be the centerpiece of the Roman New Year's celebration. **Christmas Day** (the Feast of Christ) was later stretched in Anglo-Saxon and German usage to **Christmastide**. This "season" is followed by **Epiphany** which reorients the Christian community from the meteriological darkness of winter to an emphasis upon light. Believers were able to live in a "spiritual" reality that was opposite of the physical perceptions of their universe. As Spring approaches and the agricultural societies of Europe and Asia turned to planting, **Lent** emerged. This time of recovery and renewal easily provided opportunity for pilgrimages, acts of self-sacrifice, and the practice of spiritual disciplines. Lent culminates in Holy or Passion Week that marks the last week of the earthly life of Jesus from his triumphal entry into Jerusalem on Palm Sunday to **Easter,** the great Holy Day of the Christian Year that celebrates the Resurrection of Jesus Christ from the dead.

Like Christmastide, Easter has been stretched over the centuries into Eastertide, a period of 7 weeks, also called the Season of **Pentecost**. Following Eastertide is Pentecost Sunday (also known as Whitsun), a celebration of the

Holy Spirit and the birth of the Christian Church, commensurate with the Jewish Feast of Weeks. Pentecost occurs 50 days after Passover. After Pentecost, the calendar moves to acknowledge the work months of the agricultural cycle, later referred to in Christian liturgical usage, "ordinary time." Some Protestant communions call this period Trinity Sundays or "**Kingdomtide**" as it stretches through the summer months in the northern hemisphere. As autumn approaches, there is a time of harvesting and ingathering which the Christian community has variously called **Thanksgiving** or **Harvest Home** Sundays. The cycle ends with celebrations of **All Saints Day**, commemorating the heroic figures of the Church's heritage, and **All Souls Day**, recognizing the lives of departed family members and former Christians.

Eastern Churches observe a slightly different calendar scheme. The Christian year begins on September 1 and Christmas is celebrated on January 6. In the Spring, a 10-week set of Sundays makes up Lent-Eastertide until the Sunday after Pentecost which is known as the Sunday of All Saints. In addition, there are 12 major feast days: the Nativity of Mary; the Exaltation of the Cross; the Presentation of Mary, Mother of God, to the Temple; the Nativity of Christ; the Epiphany and Baptism of Christ; the Meeting of Christ in the Temple; The Annunciation; the Transfiguration of Christ; the Dormition of Mary, Mother of God; the Lord's Entry into Jerusalem; the Lord's Ascension; and Pentecost, all recalling events in the life of Christ or the Holy Spirit.

Among many Christian churches, color plays an important aesthetic role in the recognition of seasons in the liturgical churches: green is a natural color, emblematic of growth in Christian life; red is the color of blood and fire and symbolizes zeal, and the work of the Spirit; white signifies purity, light, and rejoicing, usually associated with the Godhead; black connotes mourning and death; purple brings forth feelings of watching, fasting, and penitence, as well as the regal nature of Christ. Each season is celebrated by the appropriate color in the liturgy.

Spiritual disciplines

Like other religions of the world, Christians practice various sorts of exercises to deepen their sense of God's presence and cope with the travails and joys of life. In this context, the term "spirituality" (literally = having to do with the Spirit) covers a variety of experiential forms and varies greatly according to the categories and contexts of Christianity. Almost exclusively spiritual disciplines are understood in terms of prayer and action.

We have seen how Christians share with other religious traditions the value of prayer as communication or supplication of the supernatural. They also share a need to be devoted to God to increase their perceptions of the will of God in their lives and to know God more fully. Many religions practice asceticism, or self-denial; Christians enter into similar habits but not as mere legalistic ritual. Christians believe that spirituality is a work of the Holy Spirit in a believer that provides grace to "be" and to "do." Roman Catholics use the language of sacraments and mysticisms that are imparted to those seeking God. By continuous celebration of the Eucharist, by using Scripture and prayers, by focusing upon the lives of the past saints, by deep reflection and recitation, and by fasting and pilgrimages, one enhances the experience of God in one's life. One of the most popular devices for spiritual disciplines in the Catholic community is the use of the rosary. The rosary is attributed to a fifteenth-century religious society that was devoted to fostering devotional life. It involves oral or silent recitation to Christ and his mother, Mary, using the Psalms and/or prayers called "Our Fathers." To assist in the prayerful routine, strings of beads were used to count the prayers. A leading prayer for recitation is the "Hail Mary!"("Ave Maria") that is derived from the gospel text, "Hail Mary, full of grace. The Lord is with you. Blessed are you among women. And blessed is the fruit of your womb, Jesus" (Luke 1.28, 42). This prayer is said individually in private devotions and kneeling before a statue of the Blessed Virgin. Eastern Christians also use the "Hail Mary," though using slightly different words.

From the Middle Ages, Christians have produced manuals for pious exercises. These were among the first literature produced widely in the churches. Usually a collection of Psalms and accompanying prayers to be used by the faithful in the course of the Christian year various themes occur: sacrifice, suffering, joy, patience, etc. Those specially given to the practice of these disciplines were found in monasteries and houses for women, or attached to parish churches as "anchorites." Hildegard of Bingen, an abbess and spiritual director, composed nine such books that have enjoyed use since the twelfth century. Likewise, Ignatius of Loyola, sixteenth-century founder of the Society of Jesus, composed a manual called the *Spiritual Exercises* that is considered a primary text for spiritual disciplines. In a 4-week intensive period of "discernment," those following the Ignatian model experience contrition for their sins, a sense of personal call to follow Christ, transformation of personal attitudes, develop a compassion for the suffering Jesus, and finally the constant attainment of the love of God.[38]

Christians have made widespread use of other activities that many religions would affirm. Pilgrimages, for instance, have merit in the early and medieval church, as well as continuing into the present. One of the great attractions to Rome as a "capital" of Christianity from the second century was that it was the final resting place of two principal martyrs: Peter and Paul. Later in the reign of Constantine, his mother, Helena, was dispatched on a tour of Palestine to recover the holy sites and artifacts like the cross of Christ, and this stirred the hearts of Christians for centuries. Indeed, one of the stated goals of the Crusades was to visit the Holy Sepulchre and Jerusalem itself. Palestine became known as the "Holy Land." This activity of clergy and common people was enhanced in Europe when cathedrals were said to have accumulated relics of the apostles that could serve as cures and devotional aids. The tomb of Thomas Becket, a twelfth-century martyr, made Canterbury a site of pilgrimage for thousands from Europe and the British Isles. In more modern times, Israel is a focal point for travelers to visit the bible sites; next in priority are the churches listed in Revelation, the cities of Paul the Apostle, and lastly the sites associated with the Reformers liker Martin Luther, John Calvin, and Ignatius Loyola.

Like taking a pilgrimage to a holy site, fasting is a popular Christian discipline. Jesus went without food for 40 days in the wilderness outside Jerusalem. Fasting as a form of self-denial was a part of St. Paul's regimen of spiritual activities. Early monks like Pachomius (d.346) went without food and sometimes water for months as a statement of relying upon the strength of God alone and identifying with Jesus. In the Middle Ages, the season of Lent became a regular period of self-denial where every Christian has been encouraged to deprive themselves of some food (like meat) or activity in order to draw close to God. Sexual abstinence is related to fasting as a means of self-denial, though Paul warned that both partners had to agree for abstinence to be valid.

The apex of Eastern and Western spiritual disciplines came in the institution of the monastic life. Rooted in ancient desert religious practices, the first Christian monastic (solitary) practices were seen in the third and fourth centuries in Egypt and Palestine. Three types of monasticism developed for men and later women: "eremetical" or hermit; "laura" or solitary in community, and the true community or "coenobitic." Monks join a community and live according to a rule that encompasses all of life and throughout one's life. The ideal is to practice devotion to God as one's vocation: prayers, chants, ascetic practices like fasting, and later copying and translating the Scriptures. Always in the background is the apostolic life as seen in the Acts of the

Apostles where the disciples renounced personal property and held all things in common. The most widely accepted rules are those of St. Basil in the East and St. Benedict in the West. Both were directed toward community as a visual ideal and thus a vivid form of evangelism.[39] Several of the great Christian leaders or "doctors of the Church" were members of monastic religious communities, including Augustine, Jerome, Gregory, Hildebrand, and Martin Luther and women like Hildegard of Bingen and Therese of Avila.

While Protestant Christians do not have the heritage of sophisticated devotional manuals and disciplines, they do have concerns for practicing spirituality. Luther developed a manual for religious conversation when families gather at the mealtime called "Table Talk." He also wrote catechisms for teaching new converts and children the essentials of the faith. John Calvin's great theological treatise, *The Institutes*, was developed as a catechetical tool. In later development, the English Puritans followed a Genevan model of daily spiritual disciplines involving prayer, the reading of Scripture, self-reflection, and keeping a spiritual journal or diary. The dissenting community did follow the principle of daily reading of the Scriptures, but only in the Pietist traditions did the exercise take on a disciplined aspect.

Beginning in the post-Reformation era, there was a widely recognized need to enhance personal spirituality. It was evidenced particularly among German Lutherans and various branches of the Reformed Churches, as well as among Radical Reformed churches. Collectively known as "Pietism," the movement involved study of the Scriptures, sharing of personal spiritual activities and prayer, typically organized into small groups called "*collegia pietatis*." The widespread use of the *collegia* brought about significant renewal among the Protestant church that was in keeping with basic Protestant emphases. Among the most ardent Pietists of the eighteenth century were John and Charles Wesley in England who adopted the strategies of their Father, Samuel, and what they experienced among the Moravian Church. The Wesleyan Pietist bent produced a new Protestant tradition, the Methodists, which blended the personal piety of experiential Christianity, while at the same time holding onto the rich liturgy of the Church of England.

Modern Protestants produce both denominational and interdenominational booklets for daily devotions. These typically acknowledge some aspect of the Christian seasons and offer the user a reading from the Bible, a prayer, and some sort of suggestive story or interpretation that heightens one's individual devotional experience. Protestants understand these daily devices to be supplemental to communal worship experiences on Sundays or Lord's Day. In the

English-speaking Christian world, memorization of Scripture has also been a devotional discipline, responding to the Psalmist's injunction to "hide the word of God in one's heart that one might not sin against God."[40]

Modern Christian worship

Industrial and Postindustrial societies have brought major challenges to the routines of Christian life that were previously based upon agricultural seasons. Moreover, the rapid growth of Christianity in the Southern Hemisphere has called into question the timing of the annual holidays.

At present, Christian worship involves a mixture of rituals collected about the traditional sacramental services plus a healthy variety of praise and prayer. There are great variations across cultures, notably in the Americas and Europe. The patterns suggested in the New Testament are still influential in that prayers of a kind that bless God and offer thanksgiving from the congregation, then prayers of petition for the needs of the congregations and closing prayers are typical. Additionally, there are opportunities for the collection of financial gifts, music that usually involves singing plus choral or praise teams. A major part of the hour of worship continues to be an exposition of a passage from the Scriptures, more often the New Testament than the Hebrew Scriptures. Audience or congregational response is important in the form of an opportunity for prayer, some vivid behavior like confession or profession, or the invitation to a sacrament or ordinance.

The local congregation is still the primary unit of modern Christian worship, though not exclusively. Christians from various denominations may engage in an ecumenical service or a community may create a worship service beyond any confessional boundaries. Particularly among younger Christians, rallies or outdoor concerts and praise services are common that rely heavily upon performed music and a preacher of note, such as Pope Benedict XVI in Toronto in 2007 or the American Protestant evangelist, Billy Graham in his annual sports arena crusades. Among many denominations in Britain and North America there are annual assemblies that blend worship and administration within a given confessional body, like the Baptist Union of Great Britain, the Presbyterian General Assembly, or the United Methodist General Conference.

Christian worship has been greatly influenced by popular culture. In the past half century there has been a notable shift from the organ and piano accompaniment to guitars and drums. Congregational hymn singing and choral presentations have been superceded by small teams of singers who both perform and involve congregational accompaniment. The musical portion of worship time has become the major activity, replacing in many cases other devises like readings, prayers, and recitations. The Roman Catholic and Anglican masses have been modified to allow for the use of vernacular languages, shorter recitations, and folk music. The sound of contemporary Christian music more resembles popular culture than any continuing preoccupation with a "Great Tradition."

The Charismatic experiences within Anglican and Roman Catholic traditions have brought about revived interest in the Church and personal spiritual renewal. The term "charismatic" refers to the emphasis that these Christians place upon the presence and work of the Holy Spirit in and among believers. The Holy Spirit is believed to produce behavioral modifications (the "fruit" of the Spirit) that result in the Christian virtues, and the Spirit is manifested in special gifts like speaking in an otherwise unintelligible language, interpretation of this language, reception of specially given truths, and dramatic healings and restorations. Both the Church of England and the Roman Catholic Church have determined that charismatic Christian life and experience is valid as long as the doctrines and authority of the Church are upheld and Scripture is not violated. Generally, one can observe in charismatic worship, an occurrence of spontaneous speech, songs and litanies that praise God, and dramatic physical expressions like holding hands up to "reach toward" God, clapping hands, dancing, and the acts of anointing and laying on of hands for persons in special need. Charismatic worship is a joyous and dynamic form of Christian spiritual expression, in contrast with the more quietistic, reflective, and text-based liturgical experiences. One of the issues that charismatic renewal has raised is whether these experiences are pertinent to all Christians, or to a select group who seek them.

In the face of Western Christian absorption of popular culture, there is the bedrock of the Orthodox Churches' understanding and practice of worship. In Orthodoxy, one encounters God in special ways, for instance through icons (see Chapter 5). Because an icon is both a human product and yet seen as "full of God," it expresses to the worshiper a deeper realism. Added to the iconic art is the role of Orthodox music, the shape and layout of buildings, the use of vestments, and the domed ceilings, that all draw upon the senses to teach the reality of God. As Orthodox communities have spread beyond the traditional Middle East and Asia, their worship forms have become an attractive alternative to Protestants and particularly evangelicals who savor the recovery of the ancient traditions.

In summary

Christian spirituality is a term applied to various aspects of the Christian religion that pertain to experience in the ritual and symbols of the tradition and the deepening sense of engagement and dependence upon God. Christians believe that if God is transcendent and personal, then God may be approached and Christians may enjoy a sustained relationship with God. Prayer is thus fundamental in communicating with God. Prayer can be intimate or public, individual or collective. It is a necessity in the relationship of Christians with God.

Like other religious traditions, ritual is important to Christianity. Its earliest rituals were derived from Jewish practices and given new meanings. All believers are to be baptized, that is initiated into the Body of Christ, the Church. To commemorate the work of Christ in providing redemption, and as a bond among believers, Christians have created a ritual for the celebration of Jesus' last Passover Meal. Other minor rituals range throughout the various subgroups of the Christian faith.

The institutional Church developed strategies and devices to sanctify pagan rituals and practices. The Church devised a sacramental system to move people through the stages of life from birth to death. Included in the sacraments were recognitions of the need for controlling human sexuality and provision for successive leadership. In response to a reckoning of time that was based upon an agricultural cycle with pagan names, the Church created a Christian calendar that focuses upon the life of Christ and spiritual disciplines. In virtually every category of Christianity, there are routines and exercises that are designed to deepen one's sense of the reality of God bring a sense of fulfillment to the Christian experience. The spiritual disciplines include prayers, Scripture readings, fasting, pilgrimages, and vows for some to live in Christian communities according to strict rules.

One of the difficult questions that has emerged from within the Christian community regarding spirituality is the degree to which simply "being" a Christian is dependent upon such activity. There is an ontological, existential sense in which a person's simple faith guarantees their status before God as a Christian. The Reformers sought to restore the simplicity of "salvation by faith alone" to the spiritual expectations of being a Christian. For this reason, there has often been a perceived conflict between the Pauline position of faith alone in his Epistle to the Romans and that in the Epistle of James where good works ratify one's faith. Even Martin Luther, who was no less a figure, could not resolve the issue satisfactorily. Yet there remains a large opinion among practical theologians that one's forensic sense of being "in Christ" is evidenced by a life dedicated to God and spiritually disciplined. The Believer's Church movement, a relatively recent phenomenon in Protestantism, has further underscored the principle that understanding the fullness of Christian discipleship is a matter of adult maturity.

For further reading and study

Augustine, Tractate LXXX, 3, "The Works of St. Augustine," in Philip Schaff, editor, *Nicene and Post-Nicene Fathers*, volume 7. Peabody, MA: Hendrickson Publishers, 344, 1999.

Ayo, Nicholas. *The Hail Mary: A Verbal Icon of Mary.* South Bend, IN: Notre Dame University Press, 1994.

Baptism, Eucharist, and Ministry: Faith and Order Paper No. 111. Geneva: World Council of Churches, 1982.

Clendenin, Daniel B., editor. *Eastern Orthodox Theology: A Contemporary Reader.* Grand Rapids, MI: Baker Books, 1995.

Cowan, Marian and John Carroll Futrell. *The Spiritual Exercises of St. Ignatius of Loyola: A Handbook for Directors.* New York: LeJacq Publishing, Inc., 1982.

Delling, Gerhard. *Worship in the New Testament.* London: Dartman, Longman, and Todd, 1962.

Dudden, F. Holmes. *Gregory the Great: His Place in History and Thought,* 2 vols. New York: Russell and Russell, 1967.

A New Introduction to the Spiritual Exercises of St. Ignatius. Edited by John E. Dister. Collegeville, MN: The Liturgical Press, 1993. Foster, Richard. *Celebration of Discipline: The Pathway to Spiritual Growth.* San Francisco, CA: Harper and Row, 1978.

"General Confession," *Book of Common Prayer.* Philadelphia, PA: Prayer Book Society of Pennsylvania, 1837.

Hopko, Thomas, Father. *The Orthodox Faith: Vol. II, Worship.* New York: Department of Christian Education of the Orthodox Church in America, 1981.

Greene, J. Patrick. *Medieval Monasteries.* London: Leicester University Press, 1992.

Hahn, Ferdinand. *The Worship of the Early Church.* Philadelphia, PA: Fortress Press, 1973.

Hurtado, Larry W. *At the Origins of Christian Worship: The Content and Character of Earliest Christian Devotion.* Grand Rapids, MI: William B. Eerdmans, 1999.

Jones, Cheslyn, Wainwright, Geoffrey, and Yarnold, Edward, editors. *The Study of Spirituality.* New York: Oxford University Press, 1986.

Law, William. *A Serious Call to a Devout and Holy Life*. Philadelphia, PA: Westminster Press, 1948.

Lawrence, C. H. *Medieval Monasticism: Forms of Religious Life in Western Europe in the Middle Ages*. London: Longman, 1989.

Loyola, Ignatius. *The Spiritual Exercises*. Translated by Anthony Mottola. Garden City, NY: Image Books, 1964.

Martin, Ralph P. *Worship in the Early Church*. Grand Rapids, MI: William B. Eerdmans, 1964.

Meeks, Wayne. *The First Urban Christians: The Social World of the Apostle Paul*. New Haven, CT: Yale University Press, 1983.

Noss, John B. *Man's Religions*, Fifth Edition. New York: Macmillan Publishing Co., 1974.

Smith, W. Robertson. *Religion of the Semites, With a New Introduction by Robert A. Segal*. New Brunswick, NJ: Transaction Publishers, 2002.

Wainwright, Geoffrey. *Doxology: The Praise of God in Worship, Doctrine and Life; A Systematic Theology*. New York: Oxford University Press, 1980.

White, James F. *Christian Worship in North America: A Retrospective: 1955–1995*. Collegeville, MN: The Liturgical Press, 1997.

White, James F. *The Sacraments in Protestant Practice and Faith*. Nashville, TN: Abingdon Press, 1999.

Christian Imagery and Artistic Expression

5

Chapter Outline

Unlike other religious traditions, notably Islam, Christianity has been expressed visually over the centuries in a variety of ways that has led to an appreciation of the religious tradition beyond its sacred texts. There are symbols, two- and three-dimensional representations, and behavioral expressions of Christianity that give it a rich human experience and culture. The evidences of imagery, art, and architecture have given Christianity a pervasive influence in many different cultures. Nevertheless, all Christians are careful to recognize the essentially symbolic nature of all artistic and architectural expressions, for the God of Christians and God's temple and houses are those "not made with hands."[1] The imaging of Christianity has sparked a lively debate from its earliest centuries.

Christian symbols

The number and variety of Christian symbols is great. By their nature, symbols "throw things together" and by the power of suggestion help people recall a person or event.[2] Early Christian symbols were found on monuments, in catacombs, on parchments and manuscripts, and in mosaics. One finds material objects like ploughs, axes, and chariots useful in Christian symbolism. There are applications of symbolism to water, earth, sky, ships, and animals. Among the earliest images of the Christian movement are those of a vine and a Tree of Life. Numerous writers saw the Church as a plantation, a garden planted by the Lord, which excludes weeds. As Catholic biblical scholar Jean Danielou has shown, this imagery carries forth a familiar theme from the Old Testament.[3] In some instances, there is a connection with baptismal liturgy where the plant is seen to be growing near the Jordan River, scene of the baptism of Jesus. The ancient church theologian Cyprian comingled these images: "The Church, like Paradise, includes fruit-bearing trees within her walls . . . she waters the trees from four rivers, which are the gospels, by which she dispenses the grace of baptism."[4] Likewise, as Israel was seen as a vine belonging to Yahweh, so also in the Gospel of John speaks of Jesus as the vine the Father is a steward and disciples are the branches.[5] This terminology of "planting" was picked up early in Christian literature and denotes a missionary aspect of the church. From the nineteenth century, Protestants have been fond of speaking of missions as "church planting."

Other important images in the earliest development of Christianity include water and fish. In contrast with stagnant water, "living water" is frequently associated with the Holy Spirit. By living water, writers drew attention to water from a spring, or running water. Living water could be channeled through conduits to basins or pools but the source was always fresh. In the Old Testament, living water is a symbol of God as the source of life, and in the New Testament it devolves to the Spirit who comes to the believer at baptism after cleansing in water. In a remarkable passage, Jesus said, "If any man thirsts, let him come to me and drink . . . as the Scripture says Out of his belly shall flow rivers of living water."[6] Early monuments in the Christian community depict baptismal scenes of springs of living water and this easily transferred to depictions of Paradise rising from a tomb.

Perhaps the most famous of early Christian symbols was the fish. The early Latin theologians created an acrostic from the Greek term for fish: *ichthus* = "Jesus Christ, Son of God, Saviour." The fish was frequently connected with baptismal imagery.[7] Fishermen are associated with living waters, that is waters that are full of fish, such as in the scene where Jesus came to his disciples on the lake and directed their nets to capture swarms of fish. Closely associated with living waters and fish, was the ship itself. Here the church is seen as a ship carrying men and women through a storm. For some early thinkers

God becomes the owner of the ship and Jesus the pilot.[8] By the third century, this image became quite elaborate and included a bishop as the lookout man, the presbyters as a crew, the deacons as oarsmen, and catechists as stewards. The image came to be associated with the liturgy of ordination. One is able to draw some parallels with Noah's boat as a refuge in troubled times and Jesus' calming of the sea for his disciples in a boat. For Justin Martyr (c.100–165 CE), the ark was also a symbol of salvation.[9]

During the Middle Ages and after, a recognized set of symbols came into usage, particularly with the building of large, elaborate stone church edifices in Europe. Stonemasons captured the symbols in carvings and glass artists blended them into the stained glass windows. The purpose was the same: to instruct seekers and remind the faithful of the events and personalities pertinent to the Christian tradition. The Trinity, for instance, was depicted in three ways: an all-seeing eye or a hand in a circle for God as Father; Jesus as the good shepherd, the sun of righteousness, Lamb of God, or King of Kings; a descending dove or a flame of fire for the Holy Spirit. The three-in-oneness aspect of the Trinity has been seen as concentric circles, a triangle within a circle, or the *fleur-de-lys*. One of the more unusual depictions of Jesus the Son of God as the "Pelican-in-her-Piety" inspired by St. Augustine and Thomas Aquinas. Based upon an imagined understanding of a pelican bird who sacrificially fed her young, it is found in many Christian churches.

Biblical persons also became the subjects of Christian symbolism, as did heroic figures and saints of the church. In the Hebrew Scriptures, the Book of Ezekiel describes four winged creatures and they reappear in the New Testament Book of Revelation. They are the winged man, the winged lion, the winged calf, and the eagle. Irenaeus, a third-century Christian apologist from Gaul, asserted that each could be connected symbolically to Jesus. Thus, St. Matthew was symbolized by a winged man; the eagle represented St. Mark; St. Luke was represented by a winged calf, and St. John by a winged lion. Windows, carvings, and bible covers over the centuries carry these accepted symbols in Christian usage. Next, one might well imagine the importance of the apostles. Peter has been represented by two keys or a cock; St. James by shells that connote a journey; St. Andrew by two fish or a net; St. Thomas by a carpenter's square, etc. Next in relevance were angels: Michael, Gabriel, Raphael, Uriel, Ziphiel, Zadkiel, and Japhkiel, seven archangels in all. Finally, the early Greek and Latin theologians enjoyed symbolic representation, like St. Jerome (an open bible), St. Augustine (a heart surrounded by flames), and St. Gregory (a bishop's staff and/or a sheet of music).

Christian art employs a number of sacred monograms. The Chi/Rho is perhaps the most prominent. Taken from the Greek language spelling of Christ, it employs the first two letters to signify Jesus Christ. A legend about Emperor Constantine the Great states that he employed the Chi/Rho monogram on the shields of his soldiers and won important victories. Another monogram is *IHC*, which recalls the first three letters of Jesus' name in the Greek alphabet.[10] Likewise, among Roman Catholic churches, *INRI* stands for the Latin words *Jesus Nazarenus Rex Iudaeorum* ("Jesus of Nazareth, the King of the Jews") resembling the inscription that Pontius Pilate placed on the crucifixion cross. Finally, the Greek letters Alpha and Omega are often used to denote Christ who is said to be the beginning and the end of all things.

The most characteristically Christian symbol is the cross. As one historian of the symbol of the cross has shown, the cross is perhaps the oldest symbol in the world, not originally religious and not originally Christian.[11] The original cross was likely a simple marker; later among early Aryan peoples the Sanskrit cross or Swastika was considered a good omen and appears among Hindu and Buddhist sects. Phoenicians used a Tau cross and Egyptians employed the cross as a Key of Life. Among Christians, the cross immediately recalls the crucifixion of Jesus on a tree: a symbol of tragedy. However, Jesus himself possibly suggested the cross would become a symbol, of something much different, namely redemption and life eternal. It is for most Christians a broader symbol, of hope, salvation, resurrection, and sacrifice.

There is an important sense in which reality has imitated art in the matter of the Christian cross. In the intensity of the conversion of Emperor Constantine and his fervor for Christian symbols, he commissioned his mother, Helena, to undertake a journey to the Holy Lands in Palestine to locate the sacred sites of Christianity. Aided by Macarius, bishop of Jerusalem, Helena sought to recover the original cross of Jesus. As the legend goes, she forced a local man to divulge the secret location of the cross, plus the added finds of the tomb and grave of Jesus. Near the buried cross were four nails and the sign that Pilate had hung over Jesus. Helena's find was supposedly ratified by miraculous healings and restorations to life of sick or dying persons. The actual wooden remains of the cross of Jesus were divided in three parts, each having a memorial church structure built to protect it in Jerusalem, Paris, and Constantinople. After the Turkish armies destroyed the Jerusalem church that held a third of the cross, its whereabouts were unknown, except that following the Crusades, bits and pieces of what purported to be the cross turned up as sacred relics across the Christian world. Whether authentic or not, these are objects of veneration and devotion.

Christian crosses have taken numerous shapes and connect with related symbolic matter. There are designs of the cross according to regions, like the bulbous Russian Cross with pendent bells, or the incised Spanish design, or that associated with Switzerland that has Mary carved at its foot. The Cross of St. Andrew is an x-shaped design, supposedly the style of cross upon which St. Andrew the apostle was crucified. Celtic crosses, common in Scotland and Ireland from the sixth century, include a circle of eternity at the transept of the cross. The Latin cross is oblong with the arms shorter than the stem. A modification of this style is the Graded cross because it is elevated on three steps, symbolizing the theological virtues. Next in popularity is the Greek cross whose arms are of equal length. There are, according to one source, over 250 styles of the Christian cross.[12] If a cross has a figure of Jesus connected to it, it is called a crucifix. After the fifth century, various artistic forms of Jesus were placed on the crucifix in various degrees of clothing. The figure of Jesus was carved as an attenuated figure with a drooping head that carried a crown of thorns. The crucifix is common among Roman Catholic and some Protestant churches, signifying the continual sacrifice of Christ. Since a Byzantine Council in 753 forbade the use of images, and later the use of statues and bas-reliefs were forbidden, no Greek Churches employ crucifixes.

At St. Peter's Church in Rome there is a receptacle in the dome of the church that contains a piece of Jesus' cross plus Veronica's handkerchief,[13] and a piece of the Roman soldier's spear. In a nearby Roman church is a wooden inscription plate also purported to be from the cross of Jesus. Of the four nails used to attach the body of Jesus to the cross, legends have it that Helena threw one into the Adriatic Sea to stop a violent storm, a second was molded into Constantine's imperial crown, a third into his horse's bridle, and the other one found its way into a local church custody in either France or Italy. Somewhat comically, the sixteenth-century Christian humanist Erasmus quipped that if all the cross fragments known to exist in his time were collected there would have been enough wood to build a great ship.

The cross has found its way into personal devotional aids, amulets, practices, and extraordinary events. Priests often wear crosses that signify certain aspects of their identity. Many Christians since the sixteenth century have worn pendant crosses, some of which include the form of a saint, like

St. Christopher. In the tradition of medieval magic practices, Christians may wear crosses to ward off evil spirits or protect them while in harm's way, as on a long journey. Reliquary crosses were popular in the Middle Ages as they contained bones of saints, sacred stones, and substances believed to cure diseases. The sign of the cross, by which a Christian moves the right hand from the forehead to the chest and between the two shoulders, is understood to be a greeting or a sign of spiritual power to counteract evil spirits. An extraordinary event that frequently displays the shape of a cross is the appearance of the stigmata on a devoted person's body. The stigmata are the imitation of the wounds suffered by Jesus on the cross. Crosses are frequently found on coins, denoting the Christian nature of the ruler or government, and medals cast to honor heroic persons are often in the shape of a Christian cross. Because of its origin as a Christian mission to the sick and injured during the war, the Red Cross displays a Latin Cross as its international care-giving symbol.

The vast majority of churches across Christendom have taken account of the shape of a cross in their design. The principal entrance is always to the West with the sanctuary altar at the east, traditionally facing Jerusalem or the rising of the "Sun of Righteousness." Typically at the top of the cross is the high altar. There are historically three steps up to the sanctuary, symbolizing faith, hope, and love or the Holy Trinity. At the "crossing" are the pulpit and lectern and the entrance to the chancel. Below the transepts is the aisle or nave of the church that signifies a journey, essentially symbolizing the Christian way to God. The most common symbol in interior church architecture is the cross. In the center of the church altar is a cross. A cross usually dominated the screens separating the altars from the naves of churches. Pendant crosses hang throughout churches and the parade of clergy in services is preceded by a crossbearer or crucifer who carries a processional cross. There are likely banners that depict various forms of the cross. Important persons often wear crosses in religious ceremonies: these are referred to in Christian usage as pectoral crosses. Pope Hilarius was apparently the first to wear a pectoral cross in 461.[14]

The final place that the Christian symbol of the cross is evident is in outdoor settings. For centuries, boundary crosses have marked roads that diverged and remind the Christian traveler of one's faith. The cross on the mountain in the heart of Montreal, Quebec, is a witness to the Christian origins of that city, and the Christ of the Andes in Buenos Aires, Argentina, actually a statue of Christ in the shape of a cross, is world-famous tourist attraction. Market crosses in many medieval towns mark the sites where preachers stood to address crowds outside the churches who did not regularly attend services. Royal and civic occasional celebrations were often held at the market crosses. Of course, the most common outdoor use of Christian cross symbolism is the memorial cross. These crosses, for instance brought to the British Isles in the sixth century to sanctify church burying grounds, adorn the sacred sites of royalty and valor as well as the headstones of millions of departed persons in cemeteries and mortuaries. In more modern western cultures, billboards and signage advertising the presence of Christian activities, often carry the emblem of the cross for its universal meaning.

Christian artistic expression

At first, Christians, like Jews, were wary of creating images of God. The question thus had to be answered: Are depictions or statues particularly of Jesus considered violations of the second commandment, "Thou shall not make any hand-made images?"[15] The earliest images of Jesus (second century) were of a shepherd and presented no recognizable features. After 313, in Alexandria another image appeared, that of Christ as a teacher. In the earlier pictures, Jesus was clean-shaven, while after the fourth century he is bearded. The answer was ambiguous until 843 when icons were legitimized in both sections of the Church, but sculptured figures were no longer to be employed in the East. What came forth was a variety of mediums expressing artists' conceptions of many topics: stone etchings, mosaics, frescoes, paintings, statuary, icons, and stained glass.

Perhaps the earliest examples of Christian art to appear were designs on gravestones and ossuary boxes. In Jerusalem it is quite possible that first-century Jewish-Christian etchings on ossuary boxes that may have contained the bones of apostolic era heroes, survived in Jewish cemeteries. Likewise, Roman cemeteries from the first and second centuries evince a variety of Christian symbols on marker stones. Frescoes or wet plaster paintings appeared in catacombs and later on church walls. The "Breaking of Bread" scene in the Priscillan Catacomb in Rome from the second century and the ceiling fresco at Sts. Peter and Marcellino in Rome (fourth century), the later depicting Christ as the Good Shepherd, are classic examples of the fresco medium. Jesus was frequently depicted as a handsome young man, something like the god Jupiter, with long curly hair, typical of the Roman gods in general. The best-known example of Christian fresco is doubtless the "Creation of Adam" and related biblical scenes on the Vatican Sistine Chapel, finished by Michelangelo in 1511. Along with frescoes were mosaics, a medium made from pieces of colored stone connected into a central design. It was borrowed from Roman household floor art and became quite an acceptable expression of Christian topics in the early churches. Among the most noteworthy mosaics were the Dome Mosaic of Hagios Georgios at Salonika in Greece (c.400 CE) and the extensive illustration at Madaba in Jordan where a sixth-century church floor depicts the Holy City of Jerusalem. Two of the most celebrated mosaics are "Christ Pantocrator" (Ruler of All Things) and "Virgin and Child Enthroned," both in Hagia Sophia, Istanbul.

Similar in form to mosaics is the Christian use of stained glass to create artistic expressions. Glass seems to have originated as an art form in the Carolingian Period in Europe as jewelry and trinkets. When Gothic cathedrals were devised in the eleventh century, large windows were made possible, and glassmakers combined with artists to create impressions of light that often conveyed spiritual experiences like the "Divine Light." Vertical glass panels and great Rose Windows in cathedrals depicting Christian heroes and the life of Jesus were major features of European cathedrals. The outstanding surviving example is at Chartres, France, where a 42-foot glass image of "Mary as the Queen of Heaven" is situated near a depiction of her mother, St. Anne, who is flanked by Kings David and Solomon. Smaller imitations of stained glass adorn thousands of Catholic and Protestant churches in the West and bring to life both biblical and local subjects and themes.

The earliest Christian paintings other than frescoes were on illuminated manuscripts and later as icons and wooden panels. As monks prepared copies of the scriptures, notably the four gospels, for patrons and libraries across Christendom, artists painted the beginning letters of the gospels in beautiful colors and gold leaf plus other intermittent pages of illustrations on the life of Christ. Exemplary of this medieval art were the Lindisfarne Gospels (c.698–721), the Irish *Book of Kells* (c.760–820), and the *Utrecht Psalter* (c.820–832). Illuminated gospels became one of the most highly sought treasures of the Christian community and were often the desired items when Viking Peoples plundered the Celtic monasteries.

A special form of Christian painting is the icon, usually associated with the Eastern and Russian churches. Beginning in the fifth century in Egypt, likely in the monasteries, this new, two-dimensional form of Christian art emerged. Icons are paintings on wood panels, walls, vases, and vestments of subjects like Jesus, the Blessed Virgin, the Holy Family, angels, and other biblical and historical figures that enhance Christian worship. They can adorn sacred worship space or be displayed in public. They are basically visual images, rich in color, which use human likenesses to transfigure divine qualities. An impressive example of a sixth-century icon that survived iconoclasm is "Christ Pantocreator" at St. Catharine's Monastery in the Sinai; it was a portable icon. Quite popular among the Eastern churches, icons became a difficult problem in the West because some held that the worship was actually of the artwork and not whom/what it represented. After a church-wide debate in which the Eastern and Western Churches sharply disagreed about the use of images in worship (the iconoclastic controversy), icons became a dominant feature of Eastern and Russian Christian art and devotion, considered Orthodoxy's "highest achievement." As the ancient Eastern kontakion or hymn puts it,

No one could describe the Word of the Father;
But when he took flesh from you, O Theotokos
He consented to be described,
And restored the fallen image to its former start
By uniting it to divine beauty.
We confess and proclaim our salvation in word and images.[16]

The techniques achieved in icon painting with egg tempera and various color bases led to the further development of painting as a primary medium of Christian art. Larger paintings like the sixth century "Virgin and Child in the Midst of Saints Theodore and George" at Mt. Sinai were done on wooden panels. Paintings of members of the Holy Family were commissioned both for churches and for prominent homes in the later Middle Ages and Renaissance. Some of the world's great art involves Christian subjects in paintings: Leonardo da Vinci's "Adoration of the Magi" (1481) and his "Last Supper" (1495; copies of which are found in thousands of churches in the West); El Greco's "Christ Driving the Traders from the Temple" (c.1600); Caravaggio's "Calling of St. Matthew" (1598); Holman Hunt's "Light of the World" (1854); and Salvador Dali's "Christ of St. John of the Cross" (1951).

Statuary is of course characteristic of all ancient civilizations and the Christian community has imitated a variety of styles, mostly Greek and Roman. Apparently, the first distinctly Christian statues were made for sarcophagi. The most outstanding early example of this art was that created for the tomb of Junnius Bassus, a Christian man who died about 359 in Rome. In looking at this piece, one is struck with the sculptor's interest in depicting scenes from the bible, especially the life of Christ and the careers of Saints

Peter and Paul. In the development of cathedral churches, following the iconoclastic controversies of the period 726–843, cathedral churches featured statues of the apostles, as at St. Peter's in Rome and various other Christian heroes as in Reims, France, where there are 2,000 carved figures in the cathedral facade. The reforms instituted at Cluny in the tenth to twelfth centuries are thought to have been a great incentive to statuary, in their emphasis upon glorifying God in the liturgy. An outstanding example of this art form is Gislebertus' "Eve" at Autun Cathedral (c.1130). Christian statuary took on a magnificent aspect during the Renaissance with the work of Michelangelo in his "Pieta" (1499), his "Moses" (1515) and "Risen Christ" (1519) that aspired to a sense of ideal beauty that was free of wounds or suffering; Gianlorenzo Bernini's "David" (1623); and more recently with "Christo de la Redentor" in Brazil (1931) and "Christo de la Concordia" in Bolivia (1987–1994). The Brazilian and Bolivian statues are both 33 meters in height or roughly a meter for each year of the supposed human age of Jesus.

Related to the visual arts is music, and again the influence of Christianity has been pronounced. Among the earliest forms was the Gregorian chant, sung by choirs of men and boys since the eleventh century, but originally attributed to Pope Gregory I of the sixth century. In the Renaissance (thirteenth to sixteenth centuries), the choral Mass emerged as a principal music form. Among the most beloved modern pieces of Christian music are J. S. Bach's "St. Matthew Passion" (1727), tracing the Matthean account of Jesus' last days, and G. F. Handel's "Messiah" (1742), that encompasses Jesus' birth and death. Each of these choral selections has been performed for secular as well as religious audiences. Several national anthems or songs are also Christian hymns, notably John Bull's "God Save the King/Queen" (England; 1619), Adolfe Basile Routhier's "O Canada" (Canada; 1880), Jean Sibelius' "Finlandia" (Finland; 1899), and Katherine Bates' "O Beautiful for Spacious Skies" (United States; 1904). The net result of these musical lyrics has been to attach Christian motifs indelibly to national patriotism.

Christian architecture

The most characteristically Christian structure is the church edifice, which is in itself an artistic expression of the Christian tradition. In the earliest congregations, the voluntary associations met in homes of sponsoring or leading Christians. By the second century, however, spaces dedicated to Christian work and worship began to appear. One of the earliest to be uncovered was at

Dura-Europos in Syria, dated about 231 CE. It consisted of a central meeting room, a library, an educational meeting space for catechumens, and a particular place for a bishop's chair. Across the Empire, the Roman basilicum was adapted to Christian purposes. Located centrally in villages and cities, these public meeting halls contained the space for worship and specialized purposes. The basilicas that were used for Christian meetings typically had a large assembly room, a cathedra or large chair, a pulpit for the reading of the Scriptures and leading of singing Psalms, a baptismal font, and a table for the Eucharist, or "bloodless mysteries." The table was the most Christian aspect of a Christian basilica.

With the rise of the monarchical or supervising episcopacy, bishops required a home church from which they could administer church business and celebrate important occasions in the life of the dioceses. The places where the bishops literally sat, the "cathedra," became focal churches or cathedrals. Given their ruling status and prominence among the wealthy and influential, bishops made cathedrals elaborate houses of God, passing on construction plans and projects from generation to generation. The purposes of a cathedral were varied, including a staging place for the Eucharist and other sacraments, a location of important feasts and celebrations, a house of collective prayers, a material depiction of the life of Christ and the lives of saints, a mortuary, and a home for a regional congregation. In a unique fashion, the Christian cathedrals and principal churches provided artistic expressions in two ways, as structural phenomena, and as locations of educational exhibits. Structurally, the ceilings of cathedrals were high and lifted up to portray the grandeur and awe of God. In the cathedral apses (high semicircular spaces behind the altars), elaborate illustrations of Jesus and the martyrs adorned the walls and floor mosaics, often involving artistic devices from other religious traditions, like mandorlas or body halos, believed to have originated in Buddhist art. By reflecting on the pictures, Christians could deepen their understanding of the biblical narratives, even though illiterate themselves.

The first major boon to dedicated Christian space was doubtless the role of Emperor Constantine. In his almost total embrace of the Christian religion, Constantine provided benefits for clergy and public recognition of Christianity, as we have seen in Chapter 2. More significantly in the architectural context, Constantine provided funds from the imperial treasury for the construction of magnificent edifices, particularly in ancient Rome (a new, monumental St. Peter's Church), in the vicinity of Constantinople, the New Rome, and throughout the empire in major Christian centers like Milan or

Antioch. In the key cities, he declared there should be copies of the Scriptures and this led to appropriate liturgical furnishings for the new churches, like elaborate pulpits and altars. His mother's foray into Palestine became the foundation for church edifices at all the sites associated with the ministry of Jesus.

Another major influence beginning in the eleventh century was that of Gothic architecture. Found in France, the German states and Britain, the Gothic style was erroneously believed to be derived from crude or barbarian styles in contrast with the beauty of the Romanesque era. Rightly designated by its aesthetic and structural characteristics that originated in France, Gothic became the dominant architectural style for major public building projects across Christian Europe. The style was first employed outside Paris at St. Denis, with the first full Gothic cathedral at Laon, completed in 1190. Other outstanding examples of Gothic cathedrals are at Chartres, Paris, and Reims, France; Cologne, Strasbourg, and Marburg, Germany; and Salisbury, Durham, and Canterbury, England. An important revival of Medieval Gothic occurred in England with the Cambridge Movement of the 1840s. Inspired by students of ecclesiastical architecture, these critics and revisionists were devoted to medieval piety as the apex of the Christian tradition with its emphasis upon the authority of the clergy and the priority of the sacraments. This major recovery or shift affected virtually every parish in England and many beyond in the Anglican tradition.

The structure of Eastern Orthodox churches is devoted to the single principle, "God is with us." Eastern churches have domes that symbolize the unity and comprehensive nature of the people of God under the dome of Heaven, sometimes constructed to a height of 60 meters above the floor. The interior of Orthodox churches is often inspired by the scenes in the Book of Revelation, the center of which is an altar on which Christ is enthroned both as the Holy Scriptures and as the Eucharistic meal. Surrounding the altar may be visual reminders of angels and saints who worship God, and the standing faithful Christians who constitute the living church. Eastern churches typically include a vestibule, which is thought of as the world, a nave where the people of God are, and a sanctuary where the holiest presence of God is.[17] The curtains of Hagia Sophia in Istanbul (529), perhaps the most magnificent church edifice in the world for a thousand years, illustrated the Virgin Mary, the heavenly guardian of the monarchy, in the midst of Byzantine Emperor Justinian and Empress Theodora.

Among the great treasures of Christian public witness in architecture are the churches and cathedrals of the Russian Orthodox tradition. Displaying influences from ancient Slavic temples, the Baroque Period, and the Italian Renaissance, a wide range of achievements came forward from the eleventh through the seventeenth centuries. One sees the simplicity of small, cubicular cell churches in Kievan Rus from the medieval period, the characteristic bulbous domes, and bell towers of St. Nicholas, Novgorod (1113), the six pillars and five domes of Dormition Cathedral in Vladimir (1158), the mother church of medieval Russia, to the showpiece St. Basil's Cathedral on Red Square in Moscow (1561). The onion-shaped domes on bell towers are an adaptation of the Greek domes of heaven. Illustrative of the highest architectural and aesthetic achievement in the Russian context are the domes at Zagorsk Monastery that are punctuated with stars, and the elaborate 24-domed Intercession Church at Kizhi (1714).

Across the many streams of Christianity, there are countless styles of Christian architecture, each presumably attempting to make some aesthetic statements about God, the people of God and their service. From the Old Testament, Christians have followed two models, the tabernacle and the temple. The former speaks of the immanence or presence of God where God is in the midst of people. The temple, however, emphasizes the transcendence of God. What happened in the temple became a matter of adoration and praise in a visible sacred space. In the more liturgical churches, the temple model has received greater attention, while in the Free churches where simplicity and equality before God are important theological affirmations, a tabernacle model has prevailed.[18] A significant number of churches were constructed in the British Isles between 1400 and 1800. Most were constructed of stone and tended to be fairly uniform in layout and appearance. Following Norman designs, towers were added producing the familiar grey stone rectangular buildings with steeples, spires, or towers that many consider the most beautiful Christian buildings of all western Christian designs. Presbyterian churches in Scotland and Wales tended to be less elaborate than those of the Anglicans, typically with blunt tops to their towers rather than spires with crosses at the top. With the coming of dissenter houses of worship in seventeenth-century England and Wales, a simple square meetinghouse made of wood and more permanently, stone or brick, replaced the houses in which conventicles or illegal meetings were held.

Because of the importance of education in the Protestant Christian experience, the first modifications to Protestant meetinghouses are usually the educational space for classes, meals, and meetings. In the last half century throughout the Christian world, new construction of Gothic churches has become rare, with stone worship edifices common where stone is available.

Contemporary, practical buildings characterize Protestant churches who wish to be flexible in their use of space. An unusual adaptation of the cathedral style with an affirmation of the elements of nature is the Crystal Cathedral in Garden Grove, California, completed in 1980 at a cost of USD 17 million. This edifice is constructed almost exclusively of steel and transparent glass, with giant doors that open to fresh air and a vehicular drive-in congregation that supplements its seating capacity of almost 3,000.

Christian architecture poses some intriguing problems when the congregation for which it was built ceases to be or no longer wants to occupy the space. Urban landscapes are replete with unoccupied ecclesiastical structures. In traditions where the buildings originally are consecrated (Roman Catholic, Orthodox, and Anglican), they must be deconsecrated at the end of their service. The structures, if not destroyed, are then put to a variety of uses: educational, community gathering centers, commercial establishments, and historical sites. Some church buildings metamorphose from one denomination to another, for instance from Anglican to Black Baptist or Pentecostal usages. In Russian Orthodox experience, for instance, many Orthodox churches were abandoned during the Soviet era, only to be reoccupied by dissenters. Upon the restoration of the Orthodox Church, claims have been made to return the buildings to the Orthodox Church, resulting in litigation over the property rights. All the while, the shape, windows, appointments, and steeples remain silent witnesses to Christian imagery.

In summary

For a religious tradition that is built upon strong nonmaterial impressions of God in ancient Judaism, Christianity has moved far and wide to induce devotion in its following and express its connectedness with biblical and heroic figures. The poignancy of subjects, the patronage of the community, and the desire for symbolic representation combined to assure the enduring artistic expressions of the Christian faith. In many cases the mediums and forms either established or perfected in Christian art led the techniques of entire cultures.

The construction of buildings in a distinctly Christian pattern was likewise a huge contribution of Christianity in its aesthetic sense. Domes were borrowed from Roman models to create massive worship centers. Buttresses and the use of hard stones like granite and marble led to unprecedented building projects that reached unimaginable heights. The cathedrals of the tenth to fourteenth centuries laid the groundwork for modern superstructures and the colored translucence of glass evoked deep spiritual consciousness. Monastic communities were living examples of Christian community, carefully laid out for lives of devotion, prayer, and witness. Virtually no other religious tradition exhibits as varied a sacred architectural set of styles as Christianity.

It is evident from the earliest uniquely Christian artistic expressions that Christian artists have thought of their creations as spiritual expressions. Painters like Leonardo DaVinci envision their subjects as captive to a canvas or frame, yet alive with timeless faces and multicultural adaptations. Michelangelo's statues are so finely detailed as to illustrate the work of God as Creator. Perhaps most dramatic of all is the personal, devotional relationship that icon artists have with their subjects that can be recalled in a mystical way by all who pray in sincerity.

For further reading and study

The Baptist Praise Book. Philadelphia, PA: American Baptist Publication Society, 1871.

Beckwith, John. *Early Christianity and Byzantine Art.* New York: Penguin Books, 1979.

Benson, George Willard. *The Cross: Its History and Symbolism.* New York: Hacker Books, 1976.

Christe, Ives. *Art of the Christian World A.D. 200–1500: A Handbook of Styles and Forms.* New York: Rizzoli, 1982.

Danielou, Jean. *Primitive Christian Symbols.* Translated by Donald Attwater. Baltimore, MD: Helicon Press, 1961.

DuBourguet, Pierre. *Early Christian Painting.* London: Weiderfeld & Nicolson, 1965.

Elsner, James. *Imperial Rome and Christian Triumph: The Art of the Roman Empire AD 100–450.* Oxford: Oxford University Press, 1998.

Finney, Paul C. *The Invisible God: Earliest Christian Art.* New York: Oxford University Press, 1994.

Frese-Loche, Gervis. *Art and the Art of Christianity.* Cleveland, OH: The Press of Case Western Reserve University, 1972.

Gottlieb, Carla. *The Window in Art: From the Window of God to the Vanity of Men.* New York: Abaris Books, 1981.

Hopko, Thomas, Father. *The Orthodox Faith: Vol. II, Worship.* New York: Department of Religious Education of the Orthodox Church, 1972.

Justin, "Dialogue with Trypho," chapter 138 in Alexander Roberts and James Donaldson, editors. *AnteNicene Fathers Vol. I: The Apostolic Fathers, Justin and Irenaeus.* Philadelpia, PA: Christian Literature Publishing Co., 1885 and Peabody, MA: Hendrickson Publishers, 268, 1994.

Lossky, Vladimir. *Orthodox Theology: An Introduction.* Crestwood, NY: St. Vladimir's Seminary Press, 1989.

Ouspensky, Leonid. "The Meaning and Content of the Icon," in Clendenin, editor. *Eastern Orthodox Theology: A Reader.* Grand Rapids, MI: Baker Books, 1995.

Stafford, Thomas Albert. *Christian Symbolism in the Evangelical Churches, with Definitions of Church Terms and Usages*. New York: Abingdon Cokesbury Press, 1942.

Stevenson, James. *The Catacombs Rediscovered: Monuments of Early Christianity*. London: Thames and Hudson, 1978.

Torgerson, Mark A. *An Architecture of Immanence: Architecture for Worship and Ministry Today*. Grand Rapids, MI: Eerdmans, 2007.

Van der Meer, F., and Mohrmann, Christine. *Atlas of the Early Christian World*. London: Thomas Nelson, 1958.

Weber, F. R. *Church Symbolism: An Explanation of the More Important Symbols of the Old and New Testament, The Primitive, the Mediaeval, and the Modern Church*. Detroit, MI: Gale Research Co., 1971.

White, James F. *The Cambridge Movement: The Ecclesiologists and Gothic Renewal*. Cambridge: Cambridge University Press, 1962.

Christian Hope and Finality

6

As indicated earlier in this discussion, Christianity seeks to offer an answer to the great religious questions, among which is, "Where is the future of all things?" Christianity is thus intensely teleological. The understanding of God, the inherent value of humankind, the need for restoration of the world, and the universal desire for justice are driving impulses in Christian thinking. In this chapter, we shall look at the evolving perspectives in Christian tradition: the imminent Kingdom of God in Jesus' teaching, the delay of Jesus' promises and ideals, the fulfillment in Christian eschatology of Jewish messianism, judgment of God, and the eternal estate of Christians. It should be noted at the outset that Christian understandings of the future are in many respects no less speculative than other traditions, which has led one Orthodox thinker to caution that "the Fathers have enjoined us repeatedly that we be not curious concerning the soul after death, its condition or state . . . To seek such proofs of the objects of faith is to renounce faith . . ."[1]

Jesus and the kingdom

Early in the development of Christianity, a number of sects attempted to resolve the obvious discrepancy between the teaching of Jesus that the kingdom was present or imminent, and other places in the gospel texts where he appeared to say it would come long into the future. Among the important interpreters was a Gnostic teacher from the second century, Valentinus. He taught that at a point in a believer's life, one experiences a "restoration to fullness" which causes the person to be able to perceive and experience the world differently. Valentinus placed a number of events in this category, including the resurrection and ascension of Jesus, the resurrection of believers, and the consummation and destruction of the world. This appears to be the first instance of what would later be called "realized eschatology." In the work of Rudolf Bultmann, eschatological events become individualized and experienced as stages in the life of a believer. Even more forcibly in the writing of C. H. Dodd, a twentieth-century New Testament scholar at Manchester and later Cambridge University, "realized eschatology" means that "the eschaton has entered history; the hidden rule of God has been revealed; the Age to Come has come."[2] This understanding of future events has been persuasive to many scholars because calculating timetables of future events appears to be a flawed methodology, and because it is in keeping with the highly symbolic nature of prophetic and apocalyptic language particularly in the Hebrew Scriptures and intertestamental literature.

The Kingdom of God is a central feature of the teaching of Jesus. Variously termed the Kingdom of Heaven, Kingdom of Jesus, and with respect to gender inclusive language, the Reign of God and the Dominion of God, the Kingdom of God may be defined as the righteous rule of God in human affairs. Several questions emerge when considering the meaning of the kingdom, including, its relation to the Hebrew scriptures, its attachment to the proclamations of Jesus of Nazareth, its spirituality, and its future role in the consummation of all things. Christian biblical scholars also find some interesting points of difference between Jesus and the Apostle Paul on the meaning of the kingdom. In contrast, we shall take the kingdom at face value as some sort of sovereignty that God has over the creation, rather than as a metaphor or figure of speech, as in realized eschatology. This would follow the clear consensus among Christian groups of all kinds.

If one assumes that all of the names refer to essentially the same thing, the most obvious issue with understanding the Kingdom of God is its "already but not-yet" nature.[3] In Mark's gospel, Jesus characterized the kingdom as having come near, as though spatially referring to himself.[4] In Luke's version, he spoke of it as "among you" with the context being a collection of Pharisees who were dubious about his claims.[5] But, in his parables, the kingdom clearly appeared to be future to his ministry: in Matthew 13, the kingdom is compared to sowing seed, mixing leaven with flour, a search for hidden treasure, a merchant in search of fine pearls, and a dragnet of fish, the last of which is connected to the phrase, "so it will be at the end of the age."[6] There is mystery attached to the kingdom, for Jesus told close friends and the 12 disciples that they were given "the secret of the kingdom of God."[7] Finally, in response to interrogation from Pontius Pilate, Jesus asserted that his kingdom was "not from this world . . . not from here."[8] The interpreter of Jesus' teaching is left, therefore, to conclude that there were different aspects of the kingdom for Jesus ranging from aspects of salvation in the present to the results of his ministry in healing, etc. to inner spiritual transformation. Jesus also spoke of building his church in one passage, which some interpreters have connected with his idea of a future kingdom, but he mostly taught his disciples about the qualities of the kingdom of God and the entrance requirements.

In contrast to Jesus, Paul understood the kingdom of God as future. Much of his writing on the kingdom is directed at four aspects: the connection of the kingdom to Jesus' parousia (return); the kingdom as an inheritance of the saints; and the effects of the kingdom in the present and future. Paul saw the kingdom as connected with the return of Christ to earth and a resurrection of believers. Christ is to become the reigning king of the kingdom, perhaps a kingdom associated with the Messiah. Paul further thought the kingdom belonged to God and it would be part of Messiah's work to return it to God. The final enemy to the kingdom that will be defeated is death, and no person could enter the kingdom without a resurrection body. To the churches at Rome, Colossae, and Corinth, Paul wrote of essential attributes of the kingdom: peace and joy in the Holy Spirit, cooperation among workers in the kingdom, a complete absence of immorality, and the overwhelming presence and involvement of Jesus. If Paul had any concept of a Kingdom of God in the present, it was spiritual in nature and not political or material. He was adamant that there must be a transformation of things as they are, especially the material bodies of believers: "What I am saying, brothers and sisters, is this: flesh and blood cannot inherit the kingdom of God, nor does the perishable inherit the imperishable."[9]

What the teachings of Jesus and Paul have in common is an offer of the reign of God in the present, at least in a qualitative fashion, the return of Christ to establish a kingdom, and a view of the kingdom as the inheritance of Christian believers whose bodies and moral natures will be transformed by a resurrection. In terms of the overall expectations of a Christian eschatology, one concludes that the reign of God is certain in the permanent abode of God's dominion, and that Jesus as the Son of God will reign over the dominion. As one Orthodox thinker puts it, "the Kingdom of God is a Divine Reality. It is God's presence among men through Christ and the Holy Spirit."[10] The Kingdom of God is therefore a theological foundation of Christian hope for the future.

The "delay" in Christian ideas of the consummation

Obviously, one of the central features of the Christian future is a substantial delay in God's accomplishment of his ultimate purposes. Here one finds how Christians have accommodated the course of human history from the era of Jesus to the present and beyond. Because of the problem we identified in the texts of the New Testament that taught both the imminent and future aspects of the reign of God, this thorny problem was left to be resolved by the churches.[11]

The foundation was laid in the New Testament for one explanation, namely that God "would have all persons to be saved and come to a knowledge of the truth." Jesus' mission, according to one gospel, was "to seek out and save the lost," presumably without qualification.[12] To this is added the detail from Matthew's account of the Olivet Sermon that the good news of the kingdom must be preached throughout the world before the end comes.[13] The later first century explanation offered to aging, impatient believers in II Peter 3.9, "The Lord is not slow concerning his promise, as some think of slowness, but is patient with you, not wanting any to perish, but all to come to repentance," has been applied to remaining generations of waiting believers as well. What is at stake, then, in a delayed consummation, is God's desire that the evangelical work of the kingdom run its course until all humankind has had a chance to be saved. Tertullian, a second-century preacher in Asia Minor, was the first to refer to this period or waiting as an "intermediate state."

A second explanation arose from the teaching of St. Augustine in the fifth century. He envisioned a struggle between two cities, the earthly city of man and the city of God. Written with the decline of the Roman Empire in the background, Augustine believed that "the two cities, of God and of the Devil, are to reach their appointed ends when the sentences of destiny and doom are passed by our Lord Jesus Christ, the judge of the living and the dead."[14] Rejecting literal interpretations of a thousand year reign of Christ, Augustine thought the present era of the development of the Church from the first coming of Christ to the end of the world, is coequal with the Kingdom of Christ, where Jesus' saints reign with him and the governance of the institutional church fulfills the binding and loosing powers given by Jesus to bishops.[15] The Roman Church adopted St. Augustine's interpretation and came to see its own triumph as an institution, as a fulfillment of Christian history.

A third explanation takes the details of the end times in a purely symbolic sense and does not call for a literal parousia of Jesus or the establishment of a kingdom, or a collective transferal of dominion or redeemed people to another state. Rather, with explanations of a romanticized understanding of immortality or the plasticity of a time-space continuum as believers die, they are translated into the presence of God where Jesus is. Innumerable problems arise with each of these explanations, not the least of which is the abode of the "dead in Christ" in the meantime. This has led the church to creative accommodations like in Roman Catholic teaching the idea of purgatory where believer/pilgrims are finally cleansed and made ready for eternal life or the Orthodox and Protestant explanations of an "intermediate state," where disembodied souls consciously await the resurrection and transformation of their bodies. This state is said to be a place of rest and happiness where Jesus resides in his resurrected body, a place free from corruption, decay, entropy, and pain. Some even teach that persons are aware of events on earth, but are unable to reconnect with life on earth.

In much of Christian teaching, the place of rest and happiness for persons awaiting the consummation has often been equated with "Paradise." The reason for this equation is the announcement of Jesus on the cross to one of those crucified with him, "Today you shall be with me in Paradise."[16] Generally, the term "paradise," rich with Persian meaning, pertains to a place of exquisite delight, replete with parks, gardens, and pleasure. The person in this instance receiving such an offer was in need of the entire repair that a place like Paradise could afford. The questions remain, though, was this place promised by Jesus an intermediate state or an expedited entry into an everlasting state? Or was Jesus making a symbolic statement that lacked specificity as to place and particular circumstances?[17]

Two excursi are appropriate at this point in the discussion. The first has to do with unconscious existence between the death of a Christian believer and the resurrection, again synonymous with the "delay" in Jesus' parousia or 'second coming.' For instance, the position called "soul sleep" offered by thinkers as diverse as Martin Luther, John Milton, Seventh Day Adventists, and Jehovah's Witnesses to explain the immediate state of Christian individuals at death, is dismissed by the majority of Christians. The idea of an unconscious state of being between death and judgment is held to be inferior to a conscious waiting for resurrection. In a more plausible vein for Christians is the location of the Jewish "*Sheol*," a conscious place where, upon death, rewards and punishments are handed out preliminary to the Last Judgment. In Ecclesiastes 9.10 one finds that there is no work, nor devices, nor knowledge, nor wisdom, in *Sheol* . . . ." But, there are no other details forthcoming about life in *Sheol*.

A second excursis leads in the direction of a Christian understanding of the destiny of nonbelieving persons. In the Hebrew Scriptures, Sheol merely designates the grave or broadly speaking, death. It has no necessary moral connotations. Not so with the Greek term *hades* that appears 21 times in the New Testament. *Hades* carries with it several highly undesirable aspects: punishment, fiery torment, and separation from God. Jesus himself opened a window of understanding of *hades* in his story about a hardened rich man who at death went to *hades* and encountered fiery torment (Luke 16.19–31). To many Christians, that passage suggests that there is at least a visual proximity of the impious to the pious in the intermediate state, since there was communication between the two locales. It is important to note the obvious conclusion from Revelation 20.14 where *hades* itself is cast into a Lake of Fire, as though to suggest that the intermediate state of the impious is also brought to a definite conclusion in the consummation.

Christians and Jewish messianism

While never a mainstream consensus in the global Christian community over the centuries, Christian adoption of Jewish messianic eschatology has enjoyed a significant following. In the first three centuries, it manifested itself in chiliastic commentary particularly on passages in the Book of Revelation. Messianic expectations are bound up with aspects of the kingdom, discussed above.

One next finds a significant advancement of dispensational schemata in the writings of Joachim of Fiore (c.1135–1202). A Benedictine monk and student of Scripture, Joachim identified three major epochs in history: the Age of the Father in which humans lived under the Law; the Age of the Son wherein a dispensation of grace was ushered in under the teachings of Jesus and the apostles; and the Age of the Spirit in which new religious orders would evangelize the world and inaugurate the eternal church. While the Roman Catholic Church condemned Joachim in 1255 and again in 1263 at the Council of Arles, his ideas were broadly influential in later medieval and Reformation movements.

Perhaps the most elaborate scheme in this regard was that which emerged in the nineteenth century with John Nelson Darby (1800–1882) and those in his train. Darby's "dispensationalist" approach to understanding bible prophecy was predicated upon the idea that God acts differently to different groups in different periods: to Adam; to Noah; to Moses; to the Christian Church; and in what he called the coming "kingdom age." Later, C. I. Scofield, an American lawyer-turned-bible teacher and pastor, picked up the dispensational approach and popularized it among evangelicals in Britain and North America through the *Scofield Reference Bible*, published by Oxford University Press. Still later the prophetic hermeneutic became the *sine qua non* of leading educational institutions: Moody Bible Institute in Chicago, London Bible College (U.K.), and Dallas Theological Seminary in Texas. Best-selling books have carried forth this eschatology in clever, rationalistic, and entertaining fashion.[18]

Dispensationalism assumes that there are distinct periods in God's relationship to humans. Without covering ancient history, for purposes here, the eschatological import is this: in this system there is a coming series of events that will usher in the end of time including the removal of the living church to reign with Jesus over a thousand year kingdom politically based in Israel. Following this, there will occur a final military conflict between the forces of good and evil that God will interrupt with wrath, judgment, and renewal. The cast of characters is drawn from Persian, Hebrew, Greek, and Egyptian literature and includes the Prince of Darkness, fallen angels, archangels, the antichrist, evil politicians and religious leaders, monsters, plagues, atmospheric and environmental catastrophes. The result of all of the unleashed terror will be the preparation of a permanent home for God's people in God's presence. In collecting a number of disparate passages of Old and New Testament data, included in the Dispensationalist "last days" timetable are a

7-year period of tribulation featuring sinister international treaties and conflicts, a possible supernatural removal of living Christians from the earth, and a scenario that elevates Jerusalem to become the capital of the political powers of the world. The rationale in dispensational thinking for this elaborate eschatological timetable is a complex defeat for evil in all of its forms, a vindication of God's justice in human history, a complete fulfillment of God's promises to Israel, and a cleansing of redeemed persons to live eternally in fellowship with God.

A net benefit of dispensationalist eschatology in the past century has been a growing affection between evangelical Christians and Zionist Jews. Once the lands of the bible were set free politically from the Ottoman Empire because of World War I, Jews and Christians have yearned for a restoration of a political Israel. This became a reality in 1948 and immediately Christian expositors and pastors began to create timetables for the full realization of Messiah's kingdom. Called the "Seventieth Week of Daniel's Prophecy," it is assumed that those who witnessed the beginning stages of Israel's recovery would remain until the advent of Messiah.[19] Intense archaeological work and urban preparation leading to the rebuilding of the Jerusalem temple became a recurring theme of American pastors and Zionist financiers. For several years in the later decades of the twentieth century, all that remained for the kingdom to come was the appearance of Messiah himself. Several times, however, conservative Christian bible students have been forced to recalculate their prophetic timetables in light of changing world events. Nevertheless, the urgency of a literal messianic appearance and establishment of a kingdom remains valid. This has achieved cordial relations between conservative evangelicals and the Israeli governments who look to the support of Israel from such sources against antagonistic feelings in the international community. Yet, an awkward implication of this joint yearning for Messiah's return is the evangelical Christian understanding that Jews will have to be converted to some degree to a Christian understanding of Jesus, to be validated in the eschatological scheme.

The judgment of God

In Christian eschatology, judgment represents the ethical dimension of the consummation. All of the wrong in human civilization, all of the personal failures of individuals will be accounted for in the judgment of God. Judgment in Christian schemata is complex and it precedes the reward of the eternal life.

The judgment of God is depicted as severe, searching, and terrifying in stages, and yet also as a reward for the righteous.

In Christian eschatology, the first instance of judgment is often referred to as "particular judgment." This process amounts to an immediate Divine assessment of whether faith in God is present in an individual's life: the faithful are placed in the presence of Christ, and those deemed without faith are relegated to *Sheol,* discussed above. Theologians in the Orthodox tradition believe that the first of God's judging decisions is to assign to a person's soul the appropriate place for it to abide until the Last Judgment. There are two possibilities: a state or place of light where the souls of the righteous are and a place or state of darkness where sinful souls wait. Often the parable of the virgins in Matthew 25.1–13 is used to illustrate the difference between those who have oil for their lamps and those who do not. Orthodox Church theologians also teach that one's moral standing after death is a matter of the conviction of one's own conscience in light of the gospel.[20]

Beginning in the twelfth century, Roman Catholic thought introduced the idea, if not the place of "Purgatory." Purgatory was designed to be a bridge between the ultimate rewards in the General Resurrection and the immediate need of the righteous, but imperfect dead. Unforgiven or venial sins could be "expiated" in Purgatory and the soul of the departed is readied to receive ultimate life. Prayers of the faithful are believed to have an impact upon the duration of one's stay in Purgatory and this was cause for abuse in performing masses for the dead *ad nauseum* in the Middle Ages. Once the Scholastics developed a comprehensive sacramental theology in the twelfth century that included penance, the intermediate state of Purgatory became a place to complete unfinished penance. While New Testament passages like I Corinthians 3.11–15 that speak of one's works being evaluated by a fiery ordeal that seem to precede complete salvation, can be adduced, Protestants and Anglicans basically have followed Martin Luther in rejecting Purgatory as nonscriptural and thus without authority. As much as any other source, the poet Dante Alighieri's book, *Purgatorio* (c.1305), has established Purgatory in the Christian imagination.

Following the initial (particular) judgment is the Last or General Judgment. This is described as, "the living and the dead are judged according to their works as recorded in the book of life."[21] The basis of this judgment is the works of each person, "what they had done," all the records of all the deeds of all persons of all times. The general resurrection having taken place that will have reunited each person's soul and body, the resurrected persons appear before a judgment throne and hear the verdict as a divine decision on the ultimate state of their souls and bodies. Following the accounting, intermediate states (*Sheol* and Paradise) no longer needed, the fear of death, and unrighteous persons are tossed into a Lake of Fire that invokes Mediterranean ideas of volcanic activity. The restitution of all things, the satisfaction of a holy God completed, and rewards meted out, the consummation thus nears completion. While some Christian thinkers speculate on the possible human population of Hell, most agree that the purpose of the imagery in the Book of Revelation is to present symbolically the blessed life of the dead and the possibility of eternal loss for the wicked who hopefully will modify their rejection of God in the conduct of their natural lives in light of the stark imagery.[22]

The eternal estate of Christians

Any Christian theological treatment of "last things" is fraught with at least five difficulties: the tendency to project upon what lies ahead from Christian experience in the present; the symbolic nature of eschatological discourse; the difficulty of describing future events and circumstances that have not yet occurred (at least for living persons); the problem of defining time or temporality in the context of eternality; and the highly individualistic way in which one's Christian destiny can be described. The first issue lends itself to trying to understand Scriptural data in an overly empirical way, for instance, when Jesus promised his disciples that he was going to prepare a place of domiciles for them, the empirical imagination wants to create a picture that resembles some sort of dwelling currently known to human experience. In speaking of the meaning of trumpets and archangels in the prophetic passages, familiar apocalyptic images from the first century, how do these translate into modern discourse? Similarly, it is difficult to speak with certitude of events that have not yet occurred as though they have been preconfigured. A proper futurology is needed. And with modern notions of the time/space continuum, how does one understand time and eternity: is time to be folded into eternity? Does time in human history continue to roll endlessly on? At death do humans pass from one dimension to another? Finally, perhaps under the influence of the Enlightenment, has the ultimate destiny of humankind become so personalized that the importance of human history, that the collective meaning of salvation, and the renewal of all things are lost in a strange tyranny of an individual's needs and aspirations? Catholic theologian Karl Rahner has cautioned that Christian eschatology cannot be built upon premises that the world and history simply continue indefinitely, or that corporality in time and space also define eternal life.[23]

Those problems notwithstanding, in popular and traditional discourse, Christians have deep convictions regarding the eternal or ultimate estate of being for themselves and non-Christians. A clear consensus over the centuries exists around Christians enjoying a conscious life in the presence of God as a reward for their faithfulness in this life. Non-Christians are believed to face a set of speculative destinies, including universal salvation provided by a loving God, credit for faithfulness to other than Christian religious traditions, annihilation, or an everlasting, tortured separation from God. The Hebrew Scriptures and the New Testament, both influenced by Greek cosmology and philosophy, provide key data.

From the Hebrew Scriptures, Christians draw upon several passages. First is Genesis 2.17 ". . . of the tree of the knowledge of good and evil you shall not eat, for in the day you eat of it, you shall die." This dimension of the end of the life of the first humans has accumulated moral significance in Christian thought: "the wages of sin is death . . ."; "as in Adam all die," and "It is appointed for mortals to die once . . .?" three familiar New Testament passages that connect human sinfulness with physical death. Citations: Rom. 3.23; I Cor., 15.22; Heb. 9.27. Second, there is the oft cited passage in the Book of Job that claims that the hero of the narrative knows his redeemer lives and will prevail beyond death, and that Job will see God.[24] Aside from extraordinary circumstances such as Enoch and Elijah being translated from life to life beyond, by 250 BCE Israel's rabbis concluded that there will be a resurrection of the body and that the righteous would dwell in the City of Zion (the New Jerusalem), the capital of the Kingdom of God. Anyone who did not qualify as a "righteous one" would be cast into Gehenna.

No Christian funeral would be adequate without reference to the words of Jesus in John 14: "In my Father's house are many dwellings . . . I go to prepare a place for you and if I go, I will receive you, that where I am, you will be also."[25] Many Christians clearly expect that part of their reward for trusting Jesus will be domiciles in heaven and Jesus as Risen Lord will be proximate to them. Further, the Book of Revelation (also in the Johannine community) describes a city in which the worship of God is paramount, and the presence of the Risen Christ is everywhere evident. Paul's letter to the Corinthians adds further that Christians will enjoy recognizable bodies not subject to failure, disease, or death. The New Testament terms *aionios* and *athanasios* "World without end" characterize descriptions of the heavenly estate, assuring the faithful Christian that the next state of being is an ultimate estate.

The nature of the Christian's resurrected body is not carefully defined in the New Testament. Theologians have either inferred about its nature from other passages or left it as an unanswerable issue. From the gospel accounts, Jesus' postresurrection body was a multifaceted phenomenon. At first, the Matthew account described Jesus as a kind of apparition who looked like lightning with white, radiant clothing. Later, as he appeared to various groups, he was completely recognizable as their teacher, Jesus, just as he had been perceived before his death, same age and likeness. His body was material in that he invited his disciple, Thomas, to place his hand in the wounds inflicted by the crucifixion. But, Jesus' body was also capable of transmigration from one place to another without respect to physical barriers: "the doors of the house where the disciples had met were locked for fear of the Jews, Jesus came and stood among them . . ."[26] Later in Galilee, Jesus was seen standing on the beach by the Sea of Galilee.[27] He charcoaled fish for his disciples' breakfast and served the fish with bread to them. He walked significant distances, as with the two disciples on the road to Emmaus, he celebrated a kind of Eucharistic meal, and he taught the disciples extensively in the weeks up to his ascension. The shock of his return from death, though, was apparently enough to cause some of his followers to mistake his identity or think they had seen an unearthly being. Taking the four gospel details in composite, for Christian teachers the resurrected body of Jesus became an important paradigm for the individual Christian believer's own resurrection body.

Paul also picked up this theme in his discussions, due in no small part to anxieties raised in the early churches. A common understanding among Greek philosophers was that the human soul was immortal, a quality it possessed within itself. In contrast, the Christian community held that eternal life is a gift of God through the resurrection of Jesus Christ. Further, Christians disagreed with Greeks on the matter of disembodied souls: for early Christians, the resurrection involved a reuniting of the body in a same likeness with the soul that has been at peace since death. In his correspondence with the Corinthian church, Paul engaged in a discussion wherein he made a case for a "spiritual" body, not a body of flesh, and more than a material body in all respects. Paul's teaching was an improvement on the contemporary Jewish thinking that the elements of a decayed body in the grave would be reconstituted for a resurrected body. He conceded that, like a plant seed, the old body dies and miraculously a new body in the same likeness comes forth, yet of a different substance. In the end, Christians have come around to affirm both the Divine gift of a corporeal body and an immortal soul.

The question of the resurrected body suggests some implications for understanding the nature of Heaven as a place. The new body that Christians anticipate is an example of the transformation of the whole cosmos. Logically, a body requires a place, and for Christians the place is called "heaven." In the Hebrew Scriptures, heaven is both the physical sky and the place where God is. Exceptional persons like Enoch and Elijah went to heaven and in later Jewish thought so do all righteous persons. Heaven is a place of pure waters, abundant harvests, Spring-fresh air, and ever-bearing trees. Greeks thought of heaven as a series of tiered domains, involving angels, demons, the righteous, and the gods. In the New Testament, Jesus spoke of heaven as the place where his Father is, a place to which supplications were made, and the locale of a kingdom, cognate to the Kingdom of God. Paul told of being caught up to the "third heaven," by which he meant a place of intensive experience of God. There is also the description of heaven launched in the Revelation. It is described as a "new" heaven and a "new" earth. The new heaven is urban, bright, active, a place of intense religious activity, devoid of sickness, suffering, and immorality. Heaven is said to be "new," in contrast with what the former heaven was, and exclusive to those who love God.[28] In general, heaven is a composite of Hebrew and Greek conceptions, synonymous with the afterlife or symbolic of life eternal, the ultimate destination of all Christians.

A major issue that Christians of an eschatological orientation have debated for centuries is whether the ultimate destination resembles in any way the present world. Here is where the idea of a "new earth" comes into focus. Passages like II Peter 3.10–11 have been interpreted to mean that through some cataclysmic destruction, the present earth will be destroyed. In contrast with this view, Orthodox Christians do not look for some other world that would require a second creation, but to the present world being filled with God's presence and the full realization of the Kingdom of God. They are adamant about the falsity of teaching a destruction of the present creation that God called "good."[29] Recent environmentally sensitive Christians work theologically forward from the order and delight of creation to a renewal of the earth that will continue to enjoy the unblemished blessing of God. Traditionally, Roman Catholics have understood heaven as a place, but they have stopped short of exacting definitions, preferring instead to speak of the qualities of life in what is called the "Beatific Vision."

The eternality of a place for wicked persons has troubled Christians. In one sense, such a place seems logical for the character of a just and holy God. But, that theological idea comes up against other aspects of God's character as loving and merciful. Most Christians seem to agree that God allows all people, saints, and sinners alike, to continue to exist forever. For the Orthodox Christian community, this is not a theological problem of the character of God, but the moral choices of human beings. The scriptures and the Fathers agree that those who hate God will be in hell permanently by their own choice.[30]

In summary

All major religions would agree that to summon life from a void of whatever definition only to send it back into a void, is unfulfilling and unacceptable. Consequently, the Christian tradition has achieved an elaborate idea of the consummation—the end of all things—that is unique to its outlook in some ways, and accepting of other traditions, notably the Jewish, in other ways. The key to Christian eschatology is Jesus: his teachings, his example in the resurrection, and his presence and reign in eternity.

In the face of silence of detail, Christian thinkers have emphasized certain aspects of the future, namely the realization of the Kingdom of God, a general resurrection, a final judgment of all persons, and a final estate that is characterized as fulfillment, delight, and satisfaction in the presence of God. At the same time, Christians have wrestled with the immediate destiny of the righteous and unrighteous after death, the nature of a resurrection body and a "new" cosmos, the permanent fate of those who reject God, and the arithmetic of the numbers of righteous versus those of the unrighteous. Some Christian theologians, projecting from present experiences, have created speculative schemes about literal kingdoms, Messianic rule from Jerusalem, and an eternal life that resembles life in time and space. Most theologians, however, choose to accept a large degree of mystery in eschatological matters, preferring to follow the wisdom of the early Church theologians in worshipping in silence and exercising a supreme act of faith.

In the West, and elsewhere that exhibits western Christian influence, there is a preoccupation among many Christians with the details of human destiny. Using overly rationalistic methods of interpreting both Old Testament and New Testament prophecies, and emphasizing the particularity of details of the New Heavens and Earth and Hell as described in the book of Revelation, these interpreters purport to have relatively precise understandings of the Christian idea of the world to come, for both believers and nonbelievers. This is doubtless a response to Aristotelian/scientific descriptions of the natural world projected upon the "other world." Entire systems have been devised to detail how history will conclude (and when!) and this has had a profound impact upon contemporary world events. Rather than relying upon the power of God to bring all things to pass, literalistic interpretations can lead to human efforts to hasten the end times, from encouragements to rebuild a temple in Jerusalem, to geographical identification of Israel with the ancient kingdom of David, to a demonization of political states that appear to be acting against the interests of the coming messiah or fulfilling prophecies pertaining to ancient international relations. Eschatology can become a dominant motif in Christian thought and life and even a doorway through which some people are converted to Christianity.

Because many important questions remain unanswered in literalistic interpretations of Christian eschatology, some of the resulting speculation has brought severe criticism from mainstream Christian believers. Rather than stressing Christianity as a belief system to prepare people for life after death, many contemporary Christians chose to emphasize the quality of life "in the here and now." This has produced a rich array of writing and projects focused upon world peace, justice, human rights, and care for the earth. Such emphases are one way of interpreting Jesus' promise, "I have come that you might have life, and have it more abundantly."[31]

For further reading and study

Augustine, St. *City of God*. Translated by Gerald G. Walsh, et al. Garden City, NY: Image Books, 1958. Book XXI.

Augustine. *The City of God*. Translated by Marcus Dods. Peabody, MA: Hendrickson Publishers, 1999.

Badham, Paul. *Christian Beliefs About Life After Death*. New York: Barnes and Noble, 1976.

Beasley-Murray, George R. *The Kingdom of God*. Grand Rapids, MI: Eerdmans, 1986.

Bonino, Jose Miguez. "The Condition and Prospects of Christianity in Latin America," in Cook, editor. *New Face of the Church in Latin America*. Maryknoll, NY: Orbis Books, 266–276, 1994.

Dodd, C. H. *The Apostolic Preaching and Its Development: Three Lectures*. New York: Harper and Row, 1964.

Ehrman, Bart D. *The New Testament: A Historical Introduction to the Early Christian Writings*. Third Edition. New York: Oxford University Press, 2004.

Hick, John. *Death and Eternal Life*. London: Collins, 1976.

Himmelfarb, Martha. *Ascent to Heaven in Jewish and Christian Apocalypses.* New York: 1993.

Lindsey, Hal. *The Late Great Planet Earth.* Grand Rapids, MI: Zondervan Publishers, 1970.

Pentecost, J. Dwight. *Things to Come.* Grand Rapids, MI: Zondervan, 1969.

Puhalo, Lazar, Archbishop. *The Soul, the Body, and Death.* Chilliwack, BC: Synaxis Press, 1996.

Rahner, Karl. *Foundations of the Christian Faith: An Introduction to the Idea of Christianity.* New York: The Seabury Press, 1978.

Russell, Jeffrey Burton. *A History of Heaven: The Singing Silence.* Princeton, NJ: Princeton University Press, 1997.

Spickard, Paul R. and Kevin M. Cragg. *A Global History of Christians: How Everyday Believers Experience Their World.* Grand Rapids, MI: Baker Academic, 1994.

Turner, Alice K. *The History of Hell.* San Diego, CA: Harcourt Brace, 1993.

Wilson, Stephen G., editor. *Anti-Judaism in Early Christianity,* volume 2. Waterloo, ON: Wilfred Laurier University Press, 1986.

Witherington, Ben III. *Jesus, Paul, and the End of the World.* Downers Grove, IL: InterVarsity Press, 1992.

Afterword:
Christianity as a Missionary Religion

How a small, relatively unknown religious movement in Palestine in the first century has become a global religious tradition is a significant query in our investigation of Christianity. The answer lies in its missionary character. As one of the great missionary religions of the world—Buddhism, Judaism, Christianity, and Islam—Christianity has been borne along by partisans who believe it is the exclusive way to true meaning for humanity, the sole pathway to God. Moreover, there is in the essence of Christian teaching a universality that pertains to all humanity.[1] The majority of Christians across the centuries have taken Jesus seriously at his observation/injunction, "I am the way, the truth, and the life: no one comes to the Father except by me."[2] Moreover, their perspective on other religious traditions has for the most part ranged from disinterest to open hostility. The Christian mission is to convert the world to Christianity. Historically, from a missiological perspective, the course of Christianity was marked by five paradigm shifts: its original or Jewish phase; a Hellenistic or Gentile breakthrough; the Age of Reformation;

the triumph of the Enlightenment or liberal tradition; and the last century in which indigenization has taken place.[3]

Christians have been willing to devote their lives to the task of evangelism at great personal sacrifice and even to die as martyrs for Jesus. That in itself has made a compelling case for Christianity: in 20 centuries, over 400,000 leaders and workers have been martyred in the name of Jesus Christ. Termed the "final witness," the effect of martyrdom on evangelization is profound. Because martyrdom is not sought, but experienced in the providence of God, its impact can be electrifying and persuasive. Such news spreads rapidly among non-Christians; unbelievers and even persecutors can become converts. Saul of Tarsus, the great adversary of the first generation of Christians, participated in the stoning of Stephen, and he himself was soon thereafter dramatically converted.

Jesus and the Great Commission

Taking the composite of St. Matthew's recording of the "Great Commission," the longer ending of St. Mark, plus St. Luke's first version coupled with his second version in the Book of Acts, the earliest churches heard Jesus calling for a worldwide proclamation of Jesus' teaching to the end that an unnumbered host of disciples would be enlisted to teach and live the way of Christ, in return for eternal life with God. The texts read as follows:

> Go therefore and make disciples of all nations, baptizing them in the name of the Father and of the Son and of the Holy Spirit, and teaching them to obey everything I have commanded you. And remember, I am with you always, to the end of the age (Matthew 28: 19, 20) . . . And he said to them, "Go into all the world and proclaim the good news to the whole creation (Mark 16: 15) . . . You are witnesses of these things (Luke 24: 48) . . . But you will receive power when the Holy Spirit has come upon you and you shall be my witnesses in Jerusalem, in all Judea and Samaria, and to the ends of the earth (Acts 1: 8).

The missionary commission contains several elements of interest to the Christian community. First, these are words of Jesus which carry his authority: it is the divine founder who is issuing the command. He promises personally to accompany or support those engaged in the mission. Secondly, the targeted recipients of the witness are not exclusively Jewish, but all persons: "all the world," "the whole creation," "all nations." Third, the Great Commission is an open-ended charge, "to the end of the age." Christians since the first century have applied it to themselves in each generation. Fourthly, it is not merely a conversionist Commission, but an all-encompassing educative task that reaches to virtually all of Jesus' teachings.

If in fact Jesus' ministry began within the household of Israel, the church understood a significant transition to world religious conquest. The Catholic and Orthodox traditions took it upon themselves both to evangelize tribes on their borders in the ancient and medieval periods, and also to contend over common territory on Christian borders. Later, Protestant churches would engage in territorial missions to thwart the advance of Catholicism in the colonial era as well as competing with each other to dominate new worlds. From the late eighteenth century, evangelical Christians took the commission upon themselves, above all others, to create a scenario that would hasten the actual return of Jesus Christ to establish his permanent kingdom. Coupled with the passage from Acts 4.12 that "there is no other name under heaven whereby men may be saved," Christians are convinced that the great religious quests of humanity are fulfilled in the message of Jesus, ultimately and exclusively. There is in recent decades a new category of Christian missions, "Great Commission Christians," that is defined as "Believers in Jesus Christ who are aware of the implications of Christ's Great Commission, who have accepted its personal challenge in their lives and ministries, are attempting to obey his commands and mandates, and who are seeking to influence the Body of Christ to implement it."[4]

Across the centuries of Christian witness, however, Christians have recognized the chronological and spatial limitations of the Great Commission. As Christians are faithful to proclaim the message of Jesus, there are a finite number of them at any one time who can be in a finite set of places, affecting a finite number of hearers. Given primitive modes of transportation and communication, it was not until the latter portion of the twentieth century that the Christian message could reach the earth's population at the same time. Christian communicators have seized upon this reality to claim special opportunities for the present era. The number of persons who across the eras remain unreached, plus those of a pre-Christian era who were untouched with the message of Jesus, pose a significant missiological problem for the Great Commission. Generally, some accommodation is made, such as crediting the pre-Christian era Jewish believers with "righteousness" or leaving open the possibility that God may work through other religious traditions or means to bring people to salvation. As we shall see below, the concurrent growth of other religious traditions and the seeming failure of Christianity to overtake the world's religious quests, leaves Christians to assume that the Great Commission's results are to be accounted for according to God's unknown purposes, or that Christians occupy an elite and limited group of the entire history of humanity that God wishes to save. In either case, Christians believe they have a sacred obligation to go and make disciples.

The relative success of Christian missions

The expansion of Christianity has been a source of triumphalist attitudes in the church and a subject of scholarly inquiry. One of the most useful interpretations of Christian history is that of Kenneth Scott Latourette in his seven volume set, *History of the Expansion of Christianity*, in which he sought to recount the story of the spread of Christianity to all the peoples and places where it has adherents: by winning converts among previously non-Christian peoples, through migration, by political decree, and the creation of ecclesiastical structures.[5] The growth and expansion of the tradition in the first three centuries has been the subject of much inquiry. Likewise, the differences between terms like "evangelism" and "evangelization" create a dilemma for medieval Christianity. One of the large concerns in the propagation of Christianity focuses upon the period of the Crusades. The Reformation era is variously interpreted as growth in vitality or painful division. And the global territorial conquest of missions in the eighteenth and nineteenth centuries has been linked to Western colonial expansion. We shall look at all of these in order to evaluate the nature of Christianity as a missionary religion.

The first objects of Christian witness were mostly Jews, with a scattering of non-Jewish persons. When one puts together the messianic claims associated with Jesus, his many interactions with contemporary Jewish leaders, his quotations of Jewish Scriptures, the genealogies of Jesus, the stated purpose of two of the gospels (Matthew and Mark), it is clear that Jesus' mission was first to the household of Israel. The Apostle Paul followed this same road in reaching back into his familiar racial/religious family to make converts to the message of Christ. Only when this failed did the gospel turn to non-Jews. Why did it fail? At what point did Christianity become a completely new tradition?

Major writers from Philo of Alexandria to Origen and John Chrysostom attribute the failure of the Christian mission to Israel and the separation of the Church from the synagogue. W. H. C. Frend has thus concluded that after about 100 CE there was less of a tendency for Christians to identify themselves with Israel and more of a trend to contrast Christianity and Judaism as separate religions.[6] Christian apologists were caught between their theological and organizational indebtedness to the Hebrew prophets and the synagogue, and their extreme antipathy toward Jews for rejecting Jesus as Messiah. Frend credited Marcion in the 140s with the decisive act in rejecting the relevance of the entire Old Testament to Jesus' saving work. However, Rodney Stark and others have taken up the question of the failed mission to the Jews and reached different conclusions. Using sociological approaches to the sparse data of the historical record, Stark concludes that a substantial number of Hellenized Jews, later called Diasporic Jews, actually did convert to Christianity and did so well into the fifth century. The evidence that includes archaeological remains, texts of Jewish converts, and a revisionist look at the numbers, are indeed fascinating.

Once the Christian Church was assured the support of the Roman and Byzantine states, it began to expand its territory and temporal sovereignty. Gregory the Great (Pope: 590–603) looked longingly at a map of Europe and envisioned the boundaries of Roman Christianity as coequal with those of the Roman Empire. He was keen to envelope the British Isles into Rome's orbit and sent a trusted monk, Augustine, to secure the islands for diocesan, textual, liturgical Christianity. This resulted in the Synod of Whitby in 664 where at a debate among Celtic monks and Roman theologians, the Romans won and regional Celtic forms of Christianity faded into obscurity. The Carolingian Empire spanning central Europe was yet another chapter in Christian conquest by proclamation. In the East, strategic gains were made in the ninth–tenth centuries in portions of Syria and Armenia as well as Bulgaria. Vast territorial enlargement for Eastern Christian culture took place as Vladimir I of Kievan Rus received baptism from Eastern missionaries in 988, thus bringing the future development of Russia into the ranks of Orthodoxy. A classic territorial clash between Eastern and Western Christianities occurred in northeastern Europe where Mieczyslaw's baptism in 967 brought Greek Christianity to his dukedom in Poland through marriage, but Roman rites and episcopacy were firmly established by the combined mission efforts of the pope and Saxon Emperor Otto I, and a second marriage of Mieczyslaw, by the 970s. Poland would become a staunch member of the Roman Catholic communion thereafter.

Christianity was greatly enlarged both within its borders and beyond by several mendicant or wandering groups of dedicated men and women. The first was formed by Dominic de Guzman, a Sicilian monk, who organized the Dominican Order or Preaching Friars. These well-educated theologians went in pursuit of heretical movements and came to concentrate on ministry in the universities. A second group were the Franciscans, or Friars Minor who adopted a life of poverty and went about in groups of two, preaching, singing, identifying with peasants and helping with sick persons. Their founder, Francis of Assisi, was dedicated personally to imitating the life of Christ. A third group, the Order of the Friars of the Blessed Virgin (the Carmelites), were semimonastic, living lives of prayer, fasting, and benevolence, but engaged in pastoral care and teaching. The fourth group was the Order of Friars Hermits of St. Augustine, the Austin Friars, who were licensed to preaching and the study of the Bible. Much later in the sixteenth century, the Society of Jesus, or Jesuit Order was formed to develop a suitable defense of Catholic Christianity in light of the claims of Protestant reformers. These groups, plus a host of smaller orders of mendicants, were thus committed to propagating Christianity by the spoken word and a distinct lifestyle. It was through these friar groups that much of the work of global evangelization was accomplished from the eleventh century through the colonization of the Americas and the entry of Catholic Christianity into the Orient. These movements were often competitive with each other and quite intolerant of Protestant or evangelical missions, representing a strictly Roman version of the tradition. A strong monastic tradition in Eastern Orthodoxy followed the rivers into the Steppes creating vibrant communities and centers of learning.

At best, the new streams of Christianity that appeared in the various confessions of the Reformations spread according to both political boundaries and evangelical witness. Politically, for instance, Lutheranism spread to the Scandinavian states, Sweden, Denmark, Finland, and Norway, with Lutheran churches planted in the Baltic States and Poland. In contrast, the Reformed Churches, begun by Zwingli and Calvin, influenced Christian confessional growth in Switzerland, France, portions of Italy, the Netherlands, Scotland, England, and Wales. By extension, colonial New England, by the late seventeenth century, looked like an outpost of Genevan Calvinism. Various Pietist groups and/or Anabaptists settled in Russia, central and Eastern Europe, the Middle Colonies in America, and eventually in British North America. This new form of territorialism was staunchly defended until in the North American context, religious liberty forced the confessions to settle for religious coexistence.

In the era of 1900–2000, which saw the conclusion of the great colonial century, the global map of Christianity has changed rather dramatically. There have been swings of decline and upsurges of growth. For instance, in Europe, once considered the "sending" heartland of Christendom, membership decline has been pronounced: in largely Roman Catholic France, for instance, there has been a drop from 99.3% to 70.7% of the population; in Germany, home to the Reformation, from 98.6% to 75.8%; in Roman Catholic Italy, from 99.7% to 82.1%; and in Spain from 100% to 93.6%; in the United Kingdom (England, Scotland Wales, and Northern Ireland) from 97.4% to 86.2%; and in heavily Lutheran Sweden, from 98.9% to 67.9%. In contrast, in Eastern Europe, Polish Christianity has actually grown from 90% to 97.4% of the population.

In historically Eastern Orthodox territory, Russian statistics portray a dramatic decline from 83.4% to 57.4%, yet in Greece, there has been a growth from 85.2% to 94.7%, owing largely to relocation of persons from Turkey. An ancient witness in Cyprus has held its own in terms of adherents: from 99.8% to 94.1%. In Turkey, the transition to a basically Muslim country has witnessed Christian membership drop from 21.8% to 0.6%. In the Middle East, Christianity in Syria has shrunk from 15.7% to 7.8%; in Israel from 8.7% to 5.8%; in Lebanon, from 77.4% to 53%; and in Muslim Egypt, a decline from 18.6% to 15.1%.

Among North American and South American Christian communities, Mexico has slipped in membership of all Christian groups from 99.2% to 96.3%, still largely Roman Catholic; in the United States and Canada, pluralism has had an impact where Christian membership has declined from 96.4% to 84.7%, and even more dramatically in Canada, from 98.4% to 70%. In the same region, Cuban Christian membership has shrunk from 99.1% to 44.5% under a Marxist regime. Latin America, for hundreds of years a mission field of various Roman Catholic orders, in the last century has seen growth of Protestant and evangelical groups and yet an overall slight decline: Argentina from 98.3% to 92.9%; Brazil from 96.3% to 91.4%; and Nicaragua from 97.8% to 96.3%.

Africa and Asia provide a contrast with Europe and the Americas: in Ethiopia there has been growth from 38% to 57.7%, in Liberia growth from 10.6% to 39.3%, in Nigeria growth from 1.1% to 45.9%, in Angola from 0.6% to 94.1%, and Tanzania from 2.4% to 50.4% and most dramatically in Congo (Zaire) from 1.4% to 95.4%. In the Far East, in a Hindu and Buddhist context in India, Christianity represented 1.7% of the population and has increased to 6.2%; Chinese Christianity, surviving three revolutions in this era, has increased from 0.4% to 7.1%; in Thailand, the statistics show overall increase from 0.6% to 2.2%; Korean growth has been nothing short of phenomenal: 0.5% to 40.8%; while in Japan, a more modest increase, from 1.0% to 3.6%. Church life in The Philippines demonstrates a steady pattern of slight growth, 86.2% to 89.7%. In contrast, though, in Australia, largely influenced by British missions, church membership has declined rapidly in the population from 96.6% to 79.3%, while in Muslim Indonesia, the Christian population represents clear growth from 1.4% to 13.1% of the population. Statisticians are careful to point out that statistics for membership are substantially less than for mere "adherents."[7] For those counting, there were 558.1 million Christian adherents in the world of 1900 or 34.5% of the known population. In 2000, there were 1.1 billion Christians comprising 33% of the global population.[8] One summary has it that in this period of 100 years, for Christianity worldwide, massive gains have been offset by massive losses. [9]

There is a division of opinion amongst Christians about the vitality of Christianity and its territorial life among the nations. Some believe that the expansion and propagation of the faith is a spiritual process and involves often intense opposition. It is not uncommon to hear Christians express this in terms of spiritual warfare: "we wrestle not against flesh and blood, but against principalities, against powers, against rulers of the darkness of this world . . ."[10] Others believe that Christianity as a religious culture reached its natural boundaries in the early twentieth century and has had to compete less than favorably as the religion of western civilization ever since. A third position sees Christianity now in interaction with a variety of religions, and added to that, in a world of post-religious discourse. Leading missiologists, fully committed to the truth of the claims of Christianity, have lessened the emphasis upon any human efforts and refocused the theology of the Christian mission. As a South African, David Bosch, warns of a postcolonial Christianity, "our missionary successes may never be the criterion by which we assess the *misseo Dei* . . . the mission is God's work from first to last."[11]

The future of Christianity

Writers like Philip Jenkins have already noted a massive shift in the geography of Christianity in the past half century. It is toward the southern hemisphere and particularly Africa and Latin America. In Africa, the work of various traditional Protestant churches continues, but not to the extent that indigenous churches progress. The Christian Zionist churches are characterized by

rigorous moral disciplines and the Holy Spirit indigenous groups are ener-
gized by powerful outpourings of the New Testament phenomena in tandem
with traditional African religious practices and culture, a kind of "Pentecost
without Azusa." Latin American Christianity poses a mixed prospect: Roman
Catholicism is in transition from a re-Vatican II religiosity that is highly
liturgical and hierarchical to identifying with social justice concerns; Protestantism has become a predominantly middle class phenomenon and
shows signs of internal cooperation across confessional lines; Pentecostal
churches are becoming less other-worldly, with more indigenous leadership
and social concern; and there is the new phenomenon of transnational groups
and para-church workers. The latter category brings together a hodgepodge
of groups from traveling evangelists and "health and prosperity" advocates
to the "new" religious movements that live around the edges of traditional
Christianity like Mormons, Jehovah's Witnesses, Christian Science, the
Children of God, and the Unification Church of Sun Myung Moon.[12]

Another noticeable change in the global character of Christianity is the shift
to emphasize religious experience over confessionalism and even the sacraments. The great accomplishments of biblical criticism, scholastic theology,
and historical contextualization have been to produce a carefully scrutinized,
highly diverse religious tradition that will preoccupy scholars and religious
specialists for generations to come, much as ancient Egyptian or Persian
religions have. The new life in Christianity has come not from sacramental
debates or complex discussions of the dual nature of Jesus Christ, but from
converts who claim to have experienced Jesus in a way that has transformed
their lives. The leaders are typically Pentecostal churches independent of
established institutional Christianity.

As the older forms and categories of Christianity wane, the Pentecostal
and charismatic forms of Christianity are making their mark in the immediate
future of Christianity overall. With an estimated nine million new members a
year, or to put it in startling terms, 25,000 per day, Holy Spirit-filled Christians
are the growing edges, with charismatic Christians in the older categories
of churches outnumbering traditional Pentecostals. Those who count the
growth of Christianity observe that 27% of organized global Christianity is
of these types, comprising the world's largest congregations and clearly one
third of all Christian workers. Tracing their origins to 1549, David Barrett has
referred to this phenomenal growth as the permeation of global Christianity
and the penetration of the world by Christianity.[13] The leading criticism of
these groups is that conversion is their initial objective, followed by a second

experiential blessing that may last for 2–3 years, after which many seek a more substantial long-term sense of community and discipleship (an evolving door syndrome).

* * *

In its third millennium, most forms of Christianity are still of a mind that the world needs to be won to Christ, or given a Christian orientation. Protestants see this as continued efforts to preach the gospel to every individual, now through the use of every conceivable form of media: radio, television, the internet, and still through print. Roman Catholics speak of a "re-evangelization process" that typically means revisiting areas of traditional Catholic territory that have suffered losses to secularism and/or other religious traditions. Europe thus becomes a new mission field for Catholics through a new form of Christendom, as does Latin America through efforts like the Base Ecclesial Communities and accommodations to Liberation theology. The loss of hundreds of parishes and priests in the North American Catholic Church, make it also a strange mission field. Orthodox theologians, who have witness massive setbacks through ideological suppression and the expansion of Islam, speak of the church as a sacrament that all humanity is invited to participate in as society, culture, and nature itself are transformed by Christ who is both historical and eternal. For them it is not so much a proclamation, or an institutional extension, but an increased recognition of God in the world. All of Christianity is thus still mission oriented and in search of new believers.

Several problems remain, however, with a conversionist interpretation of Christianity. The premise that the experience of early Christianity is continuously repeatable, is difficult to sustain, even for evangelical Christians. Deducing principles from the experience of Christians in the Book of Acts is naïve and untenable, according to some missiologists, given cultural realities and lack of precise data.[14] To attempt to build a lay movement in a revisionist mode of moving away from a clerical or priestly orientation probably is not true to apostolic Christianity. Further, the experience of the early Christians with respect for the basic principles of Judaism, versus striking out in an entirely new direction, needs review because of the longer period of time before complete separation now known to have been the case,[15] and because of the continuing angst felt by contemporary Jews at the efforts some Christians make in proselytizing Jews. The experience of German Protestants and Jews in 1980 that resulted in the "Rhineland Declaration" that proposed a respect for the individual callings of Christians and Jews as witnesses of God together in the world more recently underscored the problem of the Christian witness to its most likely religious audience.

Evangelical Christians continue to look for adequate ways and means to enable the growth of the Christian community. One significant approach that Anglican evangelical John Stott has proposed, that of "incarnational" mission witness, has its adherents and critics. Stott's intention was to use the ideals exhibited in Jesus' becoming human, plus Paul's servant model of Christian witness in I Corinthians 9.19–22 to produce a kind of Christianity that is local and moves easily and comfortably in its setting in order to reach everyday people in normal circumstances. In this regard, Stott was responding to some of the issues of postmodern thought. His critics, however, feel that the term "incarnation" refers to a unique event in Jesus' becoming human and there is no biblical foundation for applying the metaphor to Christian witness. Terms like "contextualization" and "inculturation" are much to be preferred.[16] Historian/missiologist Lamin Sanneh has pursued this theme in arguing persuasively for historic missionary endeavor as a process primarily of "translation" in which adopting vernacular languages led to a "pluralist Christianity of enormous complexity."[17] Sanneh rightly believed in 1990 that the near future of Christianity in a pluralistic environment would be determined by how Christians embrace diversity or turn back to some sort of exclusivist cultural orientation. His assessment was correct and continues to be valid.

Ever popular metaphors and overarching themes like the Kingdom of God and the Great Commission of Jesus as bases for Christian witness are subject to intense scrutiny. Scholars disagree about whether there was any overarching theological theme in the diverse messages of Jesus that could provide an effective philosophical underpinning about the nature of human destiny and fulfillment. Further, taking literally a command or a commission to be a witness appears to be a less than fully noble reason for calling people to God's salvation: this has been a time-honored premise of missionary Christians. Christians are further divided over why the evangelization of the world's populations has not taken place. Is it because the message of the gospel is intended to affect only a privileged group? Is it due to inadequate efforts or problematic means of presenting the gospel? Was the expectation of the gospel writers that everyone would heed Jesus' command or only those who were eyewitnesses like the apostles?

Several major Christian missiologists, like, David Bosch, want to move the contemporary understanding of salvation from an exclusively personal concern for transcendent redemption to a broader definition that includes every realm of human life, including the transformation of relationships, political structures, and release from social and economic oppression. Bosch is thus pushing Christianity back toward the ultimate anthropological questions every religious tradition seeks to answer. To use his words, "the Church owes the world faith . . . the Church owes the world hope . . . the Church owes the world love." [18]

A key question for contemporary Christianity is whether, as a religious tradition, its truth claims require aggressive propagation or can Christianity exist alongside other religious traditions? What may be called evangelism to Christians is understood by other religious traditions as proselytization. There are essentially three categories of response to this issue of the "finality" of Christianity: the exclusivist position that asserts that Jesus Christ is the sole way of salvation; an inclusivist approach that allows for others outside the traditional Christian community to be included in God's saving work; and a pluralist understanding that attempts to raise the particularities of Christianity to a common ground of either spirituality or ethics that integrates Christianity with other traditions. Most Christians are probably in the exclusivist category, while a small number of theologians work on possibilities of valuing other religious traditions to one degree or another.

Paul Knitter, among several ecumenical Christian theologians, has suggested that Christianity has evolved to the point where through self-criticism and interaction with other religions, it is no longer necessary to claim finality or normativity for Jesus.[19] In theological terms, this means developing a theocentric orientation to religious inquiry, a subjective approach to seemingly thorny questions like the resurrection of Jesus, a "process" or transcendental Christology, and a priority of praxis or transformation in the formation of doctrine. Helmut Koester, Karl Rahner, Edward Schillebeeckx, Bernard Lonergran, and Raimundo Panikkar have all made major contributions to this type of "evolved" Christian theology. In the category of ethics, a number of Christian theologians have been working on a "global ethic" that would unite the several major religions around commitments to nonviolence and a respect for life, a just economic order, tolerance, equal rights and partnership between men and women. In this project, Hans Küng and Jürgen Moltmann have been especially active.

Yet another question remains, and that concerns the role of the church and the churches in the Christian mission. Was it churches or individuals that were entrusted with the gospel? In the last recorded interaction of Jesus with his disciples, he promised that the Holy Spirit would accompany the disciples in proclaiming the message that he is God's Messiah and the Savior of the world. Is it the goal of missionary Christianity to plant communities and assemblies in a given region, or call persons individually to new life in Christ? Is it possible to be an individual disciple of Jesus Christ while living in another religious subculture, such as Confucianism or Hinduism?

In summary

We now come to the point where this quest to understand Christianity began, namely in its response to the great questions of humanity. Like all other religions, Christianity must provide adequate answers to the issues of transcendence, self-worth, some plausible understanding of where humans have originated, and a worthy prospect of where the human race is moving.

Douglas John Hall, a thoughtful Canadian Protestant theologian, has underscored the need for Christians to accept the reality of the death of Christendom and get on with disestablishment of the faith from the cultural institutions that it has erected. He sees this as a blessing and he is correct. Only when Christians push back from all of the accommodations to political cultures, and they recover the spiritual dynamism of the first centuries of the Christian movement when Christianity was truly countercultural, can Christianity be revitalized globally. Christians must set aside world conquest in any sense and concentrate upon individual transformation.

An important priority for Christianity is to offer a new meaning to transcendence. In western scientific culture, people have become accustomed to empirical verification of reality. If something is real, it must be verifiable through one's sensory perceptions. It must meet the tests of verifiability in being a repeatable experience in order to be properly scrutinized. Aristotelian method has defined our orientation to the universe. This is where religion can have its greatest impact if it has any at all: in moving humankind beyond the obvious materiality to the spiritual realm from which we came, and for which one yearns. Through text and experience, Christians must find more adequate ways to demonstrate effective pathways to God. This will continue to be through the unbelievable (in Aristotelian terms!) incarnation of God in Jesus Christ. Most Christians will hold fast to the core of their tradition that "God was in Christ, reconciling the world to God, not imputing their sins to them, having committed to us the word of reconciliation."[20]

A second characteristic that will ensure the future of Christianity is the opportunity for community. Some have referred to this as "authentic community" because parishes and churches have become largely artificial and incidental associations. Associations that are based upon geography are bypassed by vocational networks and the internet, for instance. Congregations that are ruled by oligarchies and which are little able to sustain their own ranks from one generation to the next, are being upstaged by multicultural and multigenerational groups driven by ideals. Christianity will have to recover the intimacy of house churches that understand and practice virtues like love and trust.

One cannot escape the connection between Christian ethics and the effectiveness of the overall Christian tradition. A religious experience must be transforming, that is, it must change people's outlook, it must provide new pathways for life, and it must call persons to a lifestyle superior to the one to which they currently adhere. If the survival of humanity is preferable to annihilation, then peace trumps militarism as a fundamental religious principle. If sharing resources is preferred to widespread starvation and poverty, then interdependence is another principle. If conserving the rich natural resources of planet earth is preferable to wanton abuse and destruction, then stewardship of the environment becomes a vital principle. If living in community is preferable to alienation, then reconciliation to one's Creator and living peacefully within the human family is of fundamental importance.

At the heart of the Christian witness is persuasion, an appeal to human reason in recognition of human freedom. Properly unleashed, then, the good news in Jesus Christ calls all women and men to evaluate his claims.

For further reading and study

Barrett, David B., Kurian, George T., and Johnson, Todd M. *World Christian Encyclopedia, A Comparative Survey of Churches and Religions in Modern World second edition*. 2 vols. Oxford: Oxford University Press, 2001.

Bosch, David. *Witness to the World: The Christian Mission in Theological Perspective*. Atlanta, GA: John Knox Press, 1980.

Chidester, David. *Christianity: A Global History*. San Francisco, CA: Harper and Row, 2000.

Cobb, John B., and Griffin, David Ray. *Process Theology: An Introductory Exposition*. Philadelphia, PA: Westminster Press, 1976.

Cook, Guillermo, editor. *New Face of the Church in Latin America*. Maryknoll, NY: Orbis Books, 1994.

Frend, W. H. C. *The Rise of Christianity*. Philadelphia, PA: Fortress Press; London: Dartman, Longman and Todd, 1984.

Hall, Douglas John. *The End of Christendom and the Future of Christianity.* Eugene, OR: Wipf and Stock Publishers, 1997.

Jenkins, Philip. *The Next Christendom: The Coming of Global Christianity.* New York: Oxford University Press, 2007.

Knitter, Paul. *No Other Name?: A Critical Survey of Christian Attitudes Toward the World Religions.* Maryknoll, NY: Orbis Books, 1985.

Küng, Hans. *On Being a Christian.* New York: Macmillan Co., 1976.

Nock, Arthur D. *Conversion: The Old and the New in Religion from Alexander the Great to Augustine of Hippo.* Oxford: The Clarendon Press, 1933.

Oxtoby, Willard G. and Segal, Alan F. *A Concise Introduction to World Religions.* Don Mills, ON: Oxford University Press, 2007.

Sanneh, Lamin. *Translating the Message: The Missionary Impact on Culture.* Maryknoll, NY: Orbis Books, 1989.

Schillebeekbx, Edward. *Jesus: An Experiment in Christology.* New York: Crossroads, 1979.

Schnabel, Eckhard J. *Early Christian Mission: Paul and the Early Church.* Downer's Grove, IL: InterVarsity Press, 2004.

Spickard, Paul R. and Kevin M. Cragg. *A Global History of Christians: How Everyday Believers Experience Their World.* Grand Rapids, MI: Baker Academic, 1994.

Stark, Rodney. *The Rise of Christianity: A Sociologist Reconsiders History.* Princeton, NJ: Princeton University Press, 1996.

Notes

Series Preface

1. Or, as Smart (1968) put it "the study of man is in an important sense participatory—for one has to enter into men's intentions, beliefs, myths, desire, in order to understand why they act as they do—it is fatal if cultures including our own are described merely externally, without entering into dialog with them" (104).

2. As Religious Studies becomes more participatory, concerned with the faith in people's hearts, practitioners who self-identify with a faith tradition will inevitably explore questions about the status of their own faith in relation with others, thus treading on what might be regarded as theological ground. As Religious Studies professionals become involved in personal encounter, the distinction between Religious Studies and Theology becomes blurred. For some, this compromises Religious Studies as a neutral discipline. Others point out that Religious Studies can evaluate the plausibility of arguments or theological stances regarding the status of different religions without adjudicating whether they are true or false, thus remaining neutral. A confessional theologian, for his or her part, might declare a certain view correct and that others are heretical, or suspect.

Introduction

1. Luke 1.3.

2. Peter Gay, *The Enlightenment: An Interpretation: The Rise of Modern Paganism* (London: Widenfeld and Nicolson, 1966), 257ff.

3. Gay, *The Enlightenment: An Interpretation*, 368.

4. H. Richard Niebuhr, *The Social Sources of Denominationalism* (New York: Henry Holt and Company, 1929), 25.

5. Gustavo Gutierrez, *Theology of Liberation: History, Politics, and Salvation* (Maryknoll, NY: Orbis Books, 1988), 3.

6. John Millbank, *Theology and Social Theory: Beyond Secular Reason* (Oxford: Blackwell, 1990), 4; 139.

7. John B. Cobb, Jr., and David Ray Griffin, *Process Theology: An Introductory Exposition* (Louisville, KY: Westminster John Knox Press, 1976), 54.

Chapter 1

1. The Septuagint was a translation of the Hebrew Scriptures made in Alexandria about the third century BCE and popularly used in Palestine during the time of Jesus.
2. Matthew 5.17.
3. Psalms 22.1.
4. The term "incarnation" refers to the Christian belief that as a supernatural or spiritual being, Jesus became human and lived in a physical body for his human life. After this, he reassumed a spiritual existence.
5. Ernst Wuerthwein, *The Text of the Old Testament: An Introduction to the Biblia Hebraica* (Grand Rapids, MI: Eerdmans, 1979), 49.
6. See, for instance, John Reumann, *Jesus in the Church's Gospels: Modern Scholarship and the Earliest Sources* (Philadelphia, PA: Fortress Press, 1968), 30–35.
7. John 20.30–31.
8. Paul Tillich, *Systematic Theology,* volume II (Chicago, IL: University of Chicago Press, 1963), 113–114.
9. Form criticism has been applied to the Old Testament as well and accompanied the earlier critical methods of the Documentary Hypothesis.
10. This is actually a Bultmanian term that involves the central proclamation about Jesus that unified the earliest churches.
11. The findings of the Jesus Seminar were published in *Five Gospels: The Search for the Authentic Words of Jesus* (1993).
12. Some scholars argue that some elements of the noncanonical gospels were older than those in the New Testament. See John Dominic Crossan, *Four Other Gospels: Shadows on the Contours of the Canon* (Minneapolis, MN: Winston Press, 1987), 26.
13. This is based upon the mentioning of Passover Feasts in the Gospel of John.
14. John 2.13–22.
15. John 18.36.
16. John 6.66.
17. Historians of the resurrection event have difficulty with the historicity of the resurrection because it was a unique event. See for instance, Bart D. Ehrman, *The New Testament: A Historical Introduction to The Early Christian Writings, Third Edition* (New York: Oxford University Press, 2004), 15–16.
18. Christians assume that Joseph died before Jesus' public ministry, having trained Jesus in a trade which tradition and noncanonical literature have denoted as carpentry.
19. Epistle to the Philippians 2.5.
20. John 14.10, 11.
21. In the Nicene Creed, Jesus is affirmed as "God of God, Light of Light, Very God of Very God . . ."
22. Mark 1.15.
23. Revelation 20.1–6.

24. Luke 17.21.

25. See, for instance, Don Cupitt, *Reforming Christianity* (Santa Rosa, CA: Polebridge Press, 2001), 33–41.

26. Mark 8.31.

27. Matthew 1.1.

28. Luke 24.47.

29. John 17.25.

30. Epistle to the Hebrews 8.1.

31. Matthew 16.18.

32. Luke 22.19.

33. First Epistle to the Corinthians 11.26.

34. N. T. Wright, *The Resurrection of the Son of God* (Minneapolis, MN: Augsburg Fortress Press, 2003), 225.

35. James D. G. Dunn, *The Theology of Paul the Apostle* (Grand Rapids, MI: Eerdmans, 1998), 726.

36. Epistle to the Galatians 3.24.

37. Epistle to the Ephesians 2.5, 8; Epistle to the Romans 3.28.

38. Dunn, *Theology of Paul*, 461–492.

39. Epistle to the Ephesians 1.4.

40. II Corinthians 11.22–28.

41. Epistle to the Philippians 2.5–8.

42. G. R. Beasley-Murray, *Jesus and the Kingdom of God* (Grand Rapids, MI: William B. Eerdmans, 1986), x.

43. Cupitt, *Reforming Christianity*, 134.

Chapter 2

1. Matthew 16.18.

2. Larry Hurtado, *At the Origins of Christian Worship: The Content and Character of Earliest Christian Devotion* (Grand Rapids, MI: Eerdmans, 1999), 54.

3. Cyprian, *Treatise I*: "On the Unity of the Church" in *Ante-Nicene Fathers*, volume 5, edited by Alexander Roberts and James Donaldson (Peabody, MA: Hendrickson Publishers, 1999), 423.

4. Williston Walker, Richard A Norris, David W. Lotz, and Robert T. Handy, *A History of the Christian Church*, Fourth Edition (New York: Charles Scribner's Sons, 1985), 241.

5. The Donation of Constantine was an eighth-century document purporting to have been written in the fourth century by Constantine himself in which he gave the popes his palace in Rome and sovereignty of Rome, Italy, and the West. It was found to be spurious in the fifteenth century. The Isidorian Decretals were compiled by Isidore Mercator in the ninth century and contained documents that supposedly gave the Roman popes supreme authority over all archbishops and made them free from secular control. The Decretals were shown to be forgeries.

6. Kenneth Scott Latourette, *A History of Christianity* (New York: Harper and Row, 1953), 623.

7. Alexander Schmemann, "The Missionary Imperative in the Orthodox Tradition" in *Eastern Orthodox Theology: A Contemporary Reader*, edited by Daniel B. Clendenin (Grand Rapids, MI: Baker Books, 1995), 196.

8. H. Richard Niebuhr, *The Social Sources of Denominationalism* (New York: Henry Holt and Company, 1929), 54–105; 200–235.

Chapter 3

1. Wilfred Cantwell Smith, *Towards a World Theology: Faith and the Comparative History of Religion* (Philadelphia, PA: The Westminster Press, 1981), 156–157.

2. Paul Tillich, *The Protestant Era* (Chicago, IL: University of Chicago Press, 1948).

3. Thomas Aquinas, "Fruition of Natural Desire in the Beatific Vision," *Compendium of Theology*. Translated by Cyril Vollert (London: B. Herder, 1948), 113.

4. C. S. Lewis, *Mere Christianity* (San Francisco, CA: Harper, 2001).

5. From the eighteenth century, YHWH in English translations was transposed "Jehovah" or simply rendered "Lord" from the Hebrew *Adonai*. Following the lead of German Hebraicist Wilhelm Gesenius who in 1813 in his lexicon added vowels, the conventional spelling and usage has been Yahweh.

6. J. N. D. Anderson, editor, *The World's Religions* (Grand Rapids, MI: William B. Eerdmans Publishing Co., 1968), 195.

7. The accounts referred to here are Matthew, Mark, Luke, and John, and passages in Pauline letters, plus the citation in Josephus, a first-century Jewish philosopher and historian, *Antiquities of the Jews*, 18, 3, and from the writings of Pliny the Younger and Tacitus. For Jewish, Pagan, and noncanonical Christian references to Jesus in the first three centuries, see Bart D. Ehrman, *The New Testament: An Historical Introduction to the Early Christian Writings Third Edition* (New York: Oxford University Press, 2004), 195–208; 211–213.

8. Epistle to the Colossians 1.16.

9. For instance, the appearance of a priest called Melchizedek in Genesis 14.18, the three visitors whom Abraham worshipped in Genesis 18.1–18, and the fourth personage in Nebuchadnezzar's furnace in Daniel 4.25.

10. II Samuel 23.2 and Nehemiah 9.30.

11. This creed was long attributed to the leading Nicene Church theologian, Athanasius. It was known to St. Augustine and St. Ambrose. Modern scholars, however, believe its origin is to be found in sixth-century Gaul.

12. Exceptions to this would be the ancient Arian churches that survived into the early Middle Ages and modern Unitarian-Universalist groups mostly in the United Kingdom and North America. The Churches of Christ are also noted for their lack of a strong articulation of the doctrine of the Holy Spirit.

13. Epistle to the Ephesians 1.4; First Epistle of Peter 2.5, 9.

14. Matthew 16.18.

15. Epistle to the Ephesians 2.8, 9.
16. This is actually a popular Christian reference to the Hebrew biblical Prophet, Ezekiel (33.10).
17. Reinhold Niebuhr, *An Interpretation of Christian Ethics* (New York: Harper & Brothers, 1935), 189.
18. John Howard Yoder, "Peace Without Eschatology" in *The Royal Priesthood: Essays Ecclesiological and Ecumenical,* edited by Michael G. Cartwright (Grand Rapids, MI: Eerdmans, 1994), 143–167.
19. Gore produced in 2006 *An Inconvenient Truth,* a major motion picture devoted to the problem of global warming. He received the Nobel Prize for Peace in 2007.
20. John B. Cobb, Jr., *Process Theology: An Introductory Exposition* (Louisville, KY: Westminster John Knox Press, 1976), 79.
21. Jürgen Moltmann, *God in Creation: A New Theology of Creation and the Spirit of God* (San Francisco, CA: Harper & Row, 1985), 13.
22. See First Epistle to the Corinthians 14.34.
23. A second statement was issued at the WCC Assembly in New Delhi in 1961.

Chapter 4

1. *The Study of Spirituality*, edited by Cheslyn Jones, Geoffrey Wainwright, and Edward Arnold, S. J. (New York: Oxford University Press, 1986), esp. xxiv–xxv.
2. John B. Noss, *Man's Religions*, Fifth Edition (New York: Macmillan Publishing Co., 1974), 9–11.
3. William Robertson Smith, *Religion of the Semites, With a New Introduction by Robert A. Segal* (New Brunswick, NJ: Transaction Publishers, 2002), 20.
4. Amos 5.21–22.
5. Psalm 51.17.
6. Mark 11.17.
7. Revelation 4.8, 10.
8. See Geoffrey Wainwright, *Doxology: The Praise of God in Worship, Doctrine and Life; A Systematic Theology* (New York: Oxford University Press, 1980), 16–22.
9. Noss, *Man's Religions,* 13.
10. Gerhard Delling, *Worship in the New Testament* (London: Dartman, Longman, and Todd, 1962), 114.
11. Matthew 7.7–8.
12. Epistle to James 5.16.
13. John 14.13, 14.
14. Epistle to the Hebrews 9.24.
15. First Epistle to the Thessalonians 5.17.
16. Two variants of this prayer are found in Matthew 6.9–13 and Luke 11.2–4.
17. Acts 1.14.
18. Matthew 18.19.

19. "General Confession," *Book of Common Prayer* (Philadelphia, PA: Prayer Book Society of Pennsylvania, 1837).
20. Epistle to the Colossians 4.2.
21. Wayne Meeks, *The First Urban Christians: The Social World of the Apostle Paul* (New Haven, CT: Yale University Press, 1983), 148ff; Larry Hurtado, *At the Origins of Christian Worship*, 39.
22. Ferdinand Hahn, *The Worship of the Early Churches* (Philadelphia, PA: Fortress Press, 1973), 30–31.
23. Epistle to the Hebrews 10.25.
24. Hurtado, *At the Origins of Christian Worship*, 55.
25. Meeks, *The First Urban Christians*, 157.
26. Matthew 28.19, 20; Mark 16.16.
27. Acts 28.8.
28. Meeks, *The First Urban Christians*, 162–163.
29. James F. White, *The Sacraments in Protestant Practice and Faith* (Nashville, TN: Abingdon Press, 1999), 15.
30. Anglican Christians understand sacraments as "badges or tokens of profession . . . sure witnesses and effectual signs of grace" (1563 Articles of Religion, Art. XXV); those in the Reformed Tradition, as "holy signs and seals of the covenant of grace . . . instituted by God . . . [in which] there is a spiritual relation" (1646 Westminster Confession, Art. XXVII), and even some Baptists speak of them as divine mysteries and ministries that bind believers to Christ (the terms "covenant of grace" and "ingrafting into Christ" are used in the 1679 Orthodox Creed, Art. XXVIII).
31. See *Baptism, Eucharist, and Ministry: Faith and Order Paper No. 111* (Geneva: World Council of Churches, 1982), 4.
32. First Letter to the Corinthians 11.26.
33. Augustine, Tractate LXXX, 3, "The Works of St. Augustine" in *Nicene and Post-Nicene Fathers*, volume 7, edited by Philip Schaff (Peabody, MA: Hendrickson Publishers, 1999), 344.
34. F. Holmes Dudden, *Gregory the Great: His Place in History and Thought*, 2 vols. (New York: Russell and Russell, 1967), II: 416.
35. Father Thomas Hopko, *The Orthodox Faith: Vol. II, Worship* (New York: Department of Christian Education of the Orthodox Church in America, 1981), 132–133.
36. There were eight feasts or major holidays in the life of Ancient Israel: Passover; Unleavened Bread; First Fruits; Wave Loaves or Weeks; Trumpets; Day of Atonement; Tabernacles; Purim. The Christian tradition carried over only two: Passover and Weeks.
37. Roman and Barbarian celebrations included *Dies Natalis Solis Invicti*, Lupercalia, Saturnalia, Yule, Imboc, Midsummer, Harvest, and Winternights.
38. Marian Cowan and John Carroll Futrell, *The Spiritual Exercises of St. Ignatius of Loyola: A Handbook for Directors* (New York: LeJacq Publishing, Inc., 1982), 6–9.
39. C. H. Lawrence, *Medieval Monasticism: Forms of Religious Life in Western Europe in the Middle Ages* (London: Longman, 1989), 151.
40. Psalm 119.11.

Chapter 5

1. Acts 17.24; Epistle to the Hebrews 9.11.
2. Thomas Albert Stafford, *Christian Symbolism in the Evangelical Churches, with Definitions of Church Terms and Usages* (New York: Abingdon Cokesbury Press, 1942), 17.
3. Jean Danielou, *Primitive Christian Symbols*, translated by Donald Attwater (Baltimore, MD: Helicon Press, 1961), 28–29.
4. Cyprian, *Epistles,* 73.10
5. John 15.1–7.
6. John 7.37–39.
7. Danielou, *Primitive Christian Symbols*, 50.
8. Edward Hopper's popular gospel song of the late nineteenth century put it, "Jesus Saviour, pilot me over life's tempestuous sea . . ." Hopper was pastor of the Church of the Sea and Land in New York City and this became known as "The Sailor's Hymn." See *The Baptist Praise Book* (Philadelphia, PA: American Baptist Publication Society, 1871).
9. Justin, "Dialogue with Trypho," chapter 138 in *AnteNicene Fathers Vol. I: The Apostolic Fathers, Justin and Irenaeus*, edited by Alexander Roberts and James Donaldson (Philadelpia, PA: Christian Literature Publishing Co., 1885 and Peabody, MA: Hendrickson Publishers, 1994), 268.
10. A medieval version of this monogram interpreted the letters to stand for "Jesus, the Saviour of Mankind."
11. George Willard Benson, *The Cross: Its History and Symbolism* (New York: Hacker Books, 1976), 16–22.
12. F. R. Weber, *Church Symbolism: An Explanation of the More Important Symbols of the Old and New Testament, The Primitive, the Mediaeval, and the Modern Church* (Detroit, MI: Gale Research Co., 1971), 99–164.
13. According to Christian legends, Veronica was a woman who wiped the brow of Jesus on his way to the Crucifixion.
14. Benson, *The Cross*, 76.
15. Exodus 20.4.
16. Quoted in Leonid Ouspensky, "The Meaning and Content of the Icon" in *Eastern Orthodox Theology: A Reader,* edited by Clendenin (Grand Rapids, MI: Baker Books, 1995) 34.
17. Father Thomas Hopko, *The Orthodox Faith: Vol. II, Worship* (New York: Department of Religious Education of the Orthodox Church, 1972), 3–4.
18. Mark A. Torgerson, *An Architecture of Immanence: Architecture for Worship and Ministry Today* (Grand Rapids, MI: Eerdmans, 2007), 7–9.

Chapter 6

1. Archbishop Lazar Puhalo, *The Soul, the Body, and Death* (Chilliwack, BC: Synaxis Press, 1996), 1.
2. C. H. Dodd, *The Apostolic Preaching and Its Developments: Three Lectures* (New York: Harper and Row, 1964), 85.

3. Ben Witherington, III, *Jesus, Paul, and the End of the World* (Downers Grove, IL: InterVarsity Press, 1992), 74.

4. Mark 1.15.

5. Luke 17.21.

6. Matthew 13.49.

7. Mark 4.11.

8. John 18.36.

9. First Epistle to the Corinthians 15.50.

10. Father Thomas Hopko, *The Orthodox Faith: Volume I: Doctrine* (New York: The Department of Religious Education of the Orthodox Church in America, 1981), 117.

11. See for instance the explanation offered by Bart D. Ehrman, *The New Testament: A Historical Introduction to the Early Christian Writings*. Third Edition (New York: Oxford University Press, 2004), 265–269.

12. Second Epistle to Timothy 3.7; Luke 19.10.

13. Matthew 24.14.

14. St. Augustine, *City of God*, translated by Gerald G. Walsh, et al. (Garden City, NY: Image Books, 1958), Book XXI, chapter I, 494.

15. Augustine, *City of God*, translated by Marcus Dods (Peabody, MA: Hendrickson Publishers, 1999), volume. 2, Book XX, chapter vii–x. On the binding and loosing powers, see Matthew 16.18.

16. Luke 23.43.

17. Some have argued that the meaning of Paradise in this context must be taken within the contemporary apocalyptic usage which was either a distant place beyond the oceans, soothed by a west wind but beyond storms (Josephus, II, viii, 11) or a location simply far removed from Gehenna (II Esdras 2.19). In either case, there is potential for Christian borrowing of eschatological details from other religious traditions.

18. See for instance Hal Lindsey's *The Late Great Planet Earth,* (Grand Rapids, MI: Zondervan Publishers, 1970) and the *LeftBehind* Series, produced by Tim LaHaye (1990s). Lindsey's book has sold over 30 million copies and the LaHaye's works thus far have sold over 60 million copies. Both have been featured in motion picture formats.

19. Matthew 24.34.

20. Archbishop Lazar Puhalo, *The Soul, the Body, and Death* (Dewdney, BC: Synaxis Press, 1996), 74.

21. Revelation 20.12.

22. Karl Rahner, *Foundations of the Christian Faith: An Introduction to the Idea of Christianity* (New York: The Seabury Press, 1978), 441, 443.

23. Rahner, *Foundations of the Christian Faith*, 432, 444.

24. Job 19.25.

25. John 14.2.

26. Luke 20.19.

27. Luke 21.1, 4.

28. Revelation 21.127; 22.1–7.

29. Hopko, *The Orthodox Faith*, 133–134.

30. Hopko, *The Orthodox Faith*, 112.31. John 10.10.

Afterword

1. Willard G. Oxtoby and Alan F. Segal, *A Concise Introduction to World Religions.* (Don Mills, ON: Oxford University Press, 2007), 546–547. I include Judaism in the list because of its development of a vision to "bless the nations" and its accommodation in the first century to include non-Jews racially in the synagogues beyond Palestine.

2. John 14.6.

3. See Lamin Sanneh, *Translating the Message: The Missionary Impact on Culture* (Maryknoll, NY: Orbis Books, 1989), 9–125, for a fuller discussion of this analytical model.

4. David B. Barrett, George T. Kurian, and Todd M. Johnson, *World Christian Encyclopedia, A Comparative Survey of Churches and Religions in the Modern World, Second Edition,* 2 vols. (Oxford: Oxford University Press, 2001),volume I, 28. Barrett also notes a "Great Commission Network" that includes agencies or organizations that cooperate in such endeavors.

5. See, for instance the recent surveys of Paul R. Spickard and Kevin M. Cragg in *A Global History of Christians: How Everyday Believers Experience Their World* (Grand Rapids, MI: Baker Academic, 1994) and David Chidester, *Christianity: A Global History* (San Francisco, CA: Harper and Row, 2000).

6. W. H. C. Frend, *The Rise of Christianity* (London: Dartman, Longman and Todd; Philadelphia, PA: Fortress Press, 1984), 124.

7. These statistics are drawn from "Country Tables" in Barrett, et al., *World Christian Encyclopedia,* volume I.

8. Barrett, *Encyclopedia,* 4.

9. Barrett, *Encyclopedia,* 5.

10. Epistle to the Ephesians 6.12.

11. David Bosch, *Witness to the World: The Christian Mission in Theological Perspective* (Atlanta, GA: John Knox Press, 1980), 242; 243.

12. Jose Miguez Bonino, "The Condition and Prospects of Christianity in Latin America" in *New Face of the Church in Latin America,* edited by Cook (Maryknoll, NY: Orbis Books, 1994), 266–276.

13. Barrett, *World Christian Encyclopedia,* 19. He distinguishes four groups: Neo-charismatics from 1549; Pentecostals from 1886; Charismatics among Anglicans from 1907; Charismatics among Catholics from 1967.

14. Schnabel, *Early Christian Mission: Paul and the Early Church* (Downer's Grove, IL: InterVarsity Press, 2004), volume II, 1570–1571.

15. *Anti-Judaism in Early Christianity,*volume 2, edited by Stephen G. Wilson (Waterloo, ON: Wilfred Laurier University Press, 1986); Rodney Stark, *The Rise of Christianity: A Sociologist Reconsiders History* (Princeton, NJ: Princeton University Press, 1996), 49–73.

16. Schnabel, *Early Christian Mission,* 1575.

17. Sanneh, *Translating the Message,* 6–8.

18. David Bosch, *Witness to the World,* 244–247.

19. Paul F. Knitter, *No Other Name? A Critical Survey of Christian Attitudes Toward the World Religions* (Maryknoll, NY: Orbis Books, 1985), 230–231. Knitter is prepared to accept a "mutated" Christianity in the interests of achieving a more authentic dialog that is "dialogical, pluriform, and evolutionary" (177).

20. Second Epistle to the Corinthians 5.19.

Index

160   Index